IELTS WRITING TAS
(GENERAL TRAINING)

AUTHOR: KARAMVEER SINGH
EDITED BY: DARSHAN SINGH

Published By:

FREEDOM PRESS
SCF-32, 2ND FLOOR, PHASE–5, Mohali, Pin-160059

For any suggestions, you can reach us at freedompressteam@gmail.com

or visit – https://g.page/FreedomPublishingHouse?gm

EDITION – 1

Preface

This book is meticulously designed to address the actual needs of the IELTS test takers aiming to achieve excellence in the IELTS writing module. This book includes solved 8 + Band Writing Task samples along with Top-notch Words, Phrases, Band Descriptors, Vocabulary, and Templates essential for IELTS General Writing.

You must not look to memorise the Essays and Letters given in this book, instead, try to observe the nuances and pattern of Writing Tasks. This is one of the most researched books on this subject and is collated by inputs from bestselling authors and ex-examiners.

The author of this book, Karamveer Singh is a Barrister by profession and has been in the field of IELTS for over 10 years. He has helped more than 10,000 students in achieving their desired Band score in the Writing Module at TARGET 9.

This book is edited by one of the most eminent IELTS trainers in India, Darshan Singh.

This book contains 100 solved Letters and Essays (TASK 1 & TASK 2) based on the latest IELTS General Training pattern.

INDEX

ULTIMATE TIPS FOR WRITING IELTS LETTERS

HOW TO USE THIS BOOK

The following instructions are general guidelines for writing a Letter. If you follow the rules provided in the book, you will be capable of successfully writing an impactful letter for IELTS, scholarship programs or any other competitive examinations.

I request you to carefully read all the instructions multiple times before you start preparing for your examination. The below-mentioned rules will help you write a letter according to the needs of the question.

Once you understand the instructions, you can go through the solved letters for better understanding. I recommend that after reading the instructions, you must attempt one or two questions given in the book without reading the solution. Thereafter, you can compare your answer/s with the provided answer/s in the book to evaluate your performance.

I have put together some fantastic tips to elevate your writing scores. The following are the most important points you need to focus on when writing an IELTS letter.

If we take a closer look at task achievement in the IELTS assessment criteria, you can see the examiner checks to see if your letter contains the following features:

- Purpose of the letter is presented
- Tone of the letter is fitting
- Bullet points are presented, highlighted, and extended
- The letter format is appropriate

Let's take a closer look at what each of these dot points means, and how you need to write your letter in IELTS Writing Task 1.

STATE THE PURPOSE

Start your letter by clearly stating why you are writing, and the purpose. The reason for writing your letter needs to be vivid in the opening paragraph. Make sure the purpose of the letter is in direct response to the situation outlined in the question.

Example opening paragraphs with a clear purpose presented:

Formal letter	Informal letter
Dear Sir/Madam, I am writing to express my dissatisfaction with a product I purchased recently and to request a full refund.	Dear John, I was so pleased to hear that you are planning on visiting my country, so I'm writing to give you some travel tips and advice before you book your trip.

Common IELTS General Training, Writing Task 1 situations may include:

Formal	Informal
Letter of complaint (e.g., personal, business, recent experience, product)	Letter of invitation (e.g., party, dinner, celebration)
Letter of request (e.g., refund, repair, advice, reservation)	Letter of request (e.g., asking questions, asking for advice, asking for help)
Letter of enquiry (e.g., information request, booking)	Letter of thanks or appreciation
Letter of recommendation (e.g., job, colleague)	Letter of suggestion (e.g., suggesting ideas, plans, solutions)
Letter of suggestion (e.g., suggesting ideas, plans, solutions)	

USE THE RIGHT TONE

Let's move on to the next characteristic in your letter that the examiner is looking for, the tone of your letter. The tone denotes how you write the letter, formal or informal style. The instructions in the question will give you a clue.

Begin your letter as follows:

Dear...   Informal or semi-formal: written to a friend, colleague, or someone you know

Dear Sir/ Madam   Formal: written to someone you do not know

A formal letter contains:

- Longer sentences that use passive language (be + past participle)
- Modals (e.g., The broken light needs to be fixed to ensure that the customers who use this facility have adequate visibility of their surroundings.)

An informal letter is:

- Conversational
- Can include contractions (e.g., can't) and more direct speech (e.g., Can you fix the light in the kitchen, so I don't have an accident?)

The table shows some examples of formal and informal vocabulary and structures that you can use in your IELTS General Training Writing Task 1 response:

Formal vocabulary and structures	Informal vocabulary and structures
Request	Ask
Purchase	Buy
Could	Can
Would	Will
At your earliest convenience	When you are free
Respond	Write back/ reply
Cannot	Can't
Yours sincerely/ faithfully	Best wishes/ love
Furthermore	And/ also
Can I suggest	Can I tell you
As you described above	As I mentioned before

And finally, remember that the greeting and the closing salutation of an IELTS General Training, Writing Task 1 letter needs to match the style. For example:

Dear Sir/Madam ----------------------> Yours faithfully, Yours truly, Sincerely

Dear John ----------------------> Best wishes, Love, Lovingly

INCLUDE BULLET POINTS PRESENTED IN THE QUESTION

When writing a letter as part of the IELTS General Training Writing Task 1, it is important to include the bullet points presented to you in the question.

The question in IELTS General Training Writing Task 1 will present you with:
- A situation
- Whom to write the letter to?
- What you must include in the letter (the bullet points).

All three bullet points need to be presented

Let's break down the following question.

An overseas friend wants to visit your country on holiday.
Write a letter to your friend. In your letter

- **Recommend the best time of year to visit and why**
- **Describe the types of accommodation your friend could choose**
- **Say what you would like to show your friend in your country**

Write at least 150 words

*You do NOT need to write any addresses

Begin your letter as follows:

Dear…

Look at the first bullet point and you will see it contains two elements. So, make sure you present both:
1. The best time of the year to visit
2. Why it is the best time to visit

Look at the second bullet point and you will see that you have to describe 'types' of accommodation. So, remember to watch for plurals.

3. The first type of accommodation
4. The second type of accommodation

Example for the first bullet point, covering both elements (when and why):

Most people visit Melbourne in the summer months, but I think it's far too hot then. The best time to visit is between April and June, our autumn season. It's still sunny, but much cooler and not as humid as in the summer.

STRUCTURE YOUR LETTER

The final feature to look at in IELTS General Training, Writing Task 1 is the format of your letter. A letter needs to be written using a proper format, including the following:

- A greeting (Dear sir/madam, Dear John, Dear Mr. Smith)
- The main body (consisting of paragraphs for each part of the letter)
- A closing (Yours sincerely, Yours faithfully, Best wishes, Kind regards, Love)
-

In the instructions you are told - You do *NOT* need to write any addresses – so do not include them.

This is an example of an informal letter:

Dear Andrew

Opening salutations or greetings must be included in the appropriate letter format.

I was pleased to hear that you're going to visit Brisbane, so I'm writing to give you some information to think about before you come.

State the purpose of the letter in the opening paragraph.

Most people travel to Brisbane in the summer months, but I think it's uncomfortably hot at that time of the year. Autumn is the best season, between April and June. It's still sunny, but much cooler than in summer.

The first bullet point is presented and highlighted in a separate paragraph.

At the moment, all our bedrooms are full, so, unfortunately, we can't put you up. However, there are some economical places to stay, like Airbnb, in our suburbs. You could also stay in a serviced apartment in the city centre or on the Gold Coast. There are lots of special deals online, so I'm sure you'll find somewhere affordable.

The second bullet point is presented and highlighted in a separate paragraph.

When you get here, let me be your tourist guide. I'll take you to Lone Pine Koala Sanctuary, where you can feed kangaroos and koalas. I can also drive you to the Gold Coast for a swim. To add excitement, we can visit the theme parks there too.

The third bullet point is presented and highlighted in a separate paragraph.

Looking forward to catching up

Concluding letter (rounding off statement).

Best wishes

The closing salutation must be included in the appropriate letter format.

Laurel

Your name, to make the letter look realistic.

IELTS GENERAL TRAINING TASK – 1 GRADING CRITERIA

Task achievement

Do everything you are asked to do.
Give a fully developed response.
Include/cover all the necessary points.
Write 150 words.

Coherence:
Present ideas logically.
Use structured paragraphs.

Coherence & cohesion

Cohesion:
Write in a way that points stick together,
make sense, and convey your message.
Use standard expressions & transition words.

Use a wide range of vocabulary naturally,
correctly, and fluently.
Use correct spelling.
Choose the right words (word choice)
Use the correct form of words, such as verbs,
nouns, etc. (word form)

Lexical resource

Grammar range & accuracy

Use a wide range of grammar structures.
Include different kinds of sentences – simple,
compound, complex.
Use effective punctuation.
Use correct capitalization.

USEFUL EXPRESSIONS FOR LETTER-WRITING

To complete your IELTS letter-writing task within 20 minutes, learn to use and spell common phrases and expressions correctly. Choose the correct level of formality based on your question prompt. By using these phrases, you will save time and effort and earn a higher band score. Most of the expressions below are arranged from formal to semi-formal to informal.

Apologizing
Please accept my sincere apologies for…
I am extremely sorry about…
Sorry for…

Asking for help
I'd be grateful if you could…
I would appreciate if you could…
Could you please…

Asking for information
I am writing to enquire about…
I am writing to find out about…
I would like to know about…

Closing
I look forward to hearing from you,
I look forward to seeing you,
I look forward to meeting you,

Complaining
I am writing to express my dissatisfaction with…
I am writing to express my annoyance with…
I'm not happy with…

Expressing satisfaction
I was delighted to learn that…
I was thrilled to hear that…
I was overjoyed to hear that…

Expressing concern
I am writing to express my concern about…
I was very sorry to learn that…
I was sorry to hear that…

Giving bad news
I regret to advise you that…
I regret to inform you that…
I am sorry to tell you that…

Giving good news
I am pleased to advise you that…

Useful phrases to make a complaint

I am not happy about

I want you to know that

I am writing to express my dissatisfaction with

I am writing to express my annoyance with

I am very much unhappy with

I must complain about

I feel something should be done about

I am writing to you to complain

Useful vocabulary to make an application

I am writing in relation to the advertised position of…

Please find my CV attached…

If you have any further questions please do not hesitate to contact me…

I am available between the hours of 2pm and 4pm Monday – Thursday.

I am writing to apply for the position of…

My responsibilities included….

My most recent job was…

I believe I have all the relevant experience required…

Useful vocabulary to invite or reply to an invite

I am writing you in response to your invitation

With the reference of your proposal

Please do let me know if you can make it

Thank you for your kind invite however, unfortunately

I am writing to reply to your kind invitation regarding the

Do let me know if you can make it

It would be delightful to have you here

Please RSVP as soon as possible

Useful vocabulary to advise

I am happy to advise you that

I strongly advise you to/not to

It would/might be a good idea to

The best thing for you to do is

I honestly believe it would be better to

Please do consider my advice because

In my honest opinion, I would

I would strongly suggest you consider

Useful vocabulary to apologise

I regret to inform you

I am writing to apologise

It is with my deepest regret that

I would like to apologise

I sincerely apologise for

I do apologise for any inconvenience caused

I hope that this does not cause you any problems

I would strongly suggest you consider

Useful vocabulary to make a request

Could you please / possibly

Please would you consider

Would it be possible to

Would you be kind enough to

Is there any way you could … ?

I would strongly suggest you consider

(informal) Can you ..?

(informal) Will you ..?

Useful vocabulary for informal letters

Hello / Hi name / Hi there

I was wondering if you could help me.

I'm sorry to tell you that

I should let you know that

I hope you're well

It's been ages since I've heard from you

Lots of love

Thanks very much

TASK 1

You are getting married later this year. You want to invite your friend to the wedding. Write a letter to this friend. In your letter

- *tell your friend that you are getting married*
- *tell them when and where the wedding will take place*
- *ask them to help you prepare for the wedding in some way*

Write at least 150 words

Dear Daniel,

How are you? I hope this letter finds you in good health.

I am thrilled to inform you that I am getting married, and I want to cordially invite you to attend my marriage party. As you know, I was engaged to my long-time friend Demi. So, we have decided to tie the knot on 14th February next year.

The venue of the wedding celebrations will be my farmhouse located on the outskirts of Toronto. Besides, there will be a reception party which will take place the following day. I will make all the arrangements for you from airport pick-up to accommodation. You just come here prepared to take part and enjoy in all the ceremonies.

Since you are in the flower business, I desperately seek your assistance in managing all the floral decorations at the site. I will be obliged if you could recommend some professionals for the flower arrangements.

I am eagerly waiting for you to unite us in the moments of our happiness.

Yours loving,
Justin Green

172 Words

Vocab for task - 1

- Thrilled – excited
- Desperately – urgently
- Obliged – grateful
- Floral – flowery

TASK 2

You recently went on a sightseeing tour, and you are not happy with the quality of the tour. Write a letter to the manager of the tour company. In your letter

- *describe why you selected the tour*
- *explain what you did not like about the tour guide*
- *give suggestions to the manager to improve the tour*

Write at least 150 words

Dear Sir,

I recently availed service for a full-day Bangkok city tour from your organization. I want to bring to your kind attention that the expedition was a disappointment, as it was not according to the itinerary and the allied services were lacking.

Although your excursion was highly priced in contrast to your competitors, we still opted for this since you offered an extensive tour and a meal during its course. However, it became a misery, as there was no lunch, and the guide refused to refund the amount charged for meals. We were disappointed as the tour did not cover significant attractions as mentioned in the brochure. We were not answered satisfactorily by the tour manager about the said matter. On further inquiry by the rest of the members, he explained that the attractions were closed due to the ongoing pandemic. But in the tour detail section, no such information was mentioned.

Nevertheless, I hope your representatives provide accurate and updated information in future so that prospective customers can take an informed decision according to their needs.

I expect you will give conscious thought to my recommendation and implement it immediately.

Yours sincerely,
Justin Green

196 Words

Vocab for task – 2

- Expedition – journey
- Allied – associated
- Excursion – tour
- Misery – sadness
- Conscious – aware
- Implement – put into practice

TASK 3

You recently gave a successful presentation at work. You borrowed a book from a colleague, which helped prepare you for the presentation. Write a letter to your colleague. In your letter

- *say what the presentation was about*
- *explain why the presentation was important*
- *describe how the book helped you prepare for the presentation*

Write at least 150 words

Dear Daniel,

You will be ecstatic to know that the book you lent me was instrumental in delivering my presentation. My seniors and co-workers appreciated my work for detailed and accurate information.

The topic of my project was to reflect on the positive impacts of English law in the evolution of the Indian legal system under British rule. Since this was one of the substantial steps during my promotion, it was of utmost significance to showcase my finest work to secure the coveted designation of Head of the Department. This book, written by Lord Henry, was a running commentary on the adoption of British laws in India's post-independence era.

The book contained an in-depth analysis of the far-reaching influence of English common law on the modern-day judiciary, which helped me to extrapolate similarities between both legal systems.

I am grateful for your kindness in recommending and lending this book to me for the presentation.

Yours sincerely,
Justin Green

158 Words

Vocab for task – 3

- Ecstatic – overjoyed
- Instrumental – influential / helpful
- Evolution – development
- Substantial – considerable
- Utmost – extreme / supreme
- Coveted – desired
- Extrapolate – deduce / reason

TASK 4

A neighbour recently invited you to a special party. You intended to go but could not attend at the last minute. Write a letter to your neighbour. In your letter

- *apologize for not going to the party*
- *explain why you didn't go*
- *suggest a way to make up for missing the part*

Write at least 150 words

Dear Daniel,

I want to extend my heartiest congratulations on your promotion to the desired position at your company. I am overjoyed at your achievement.

Everyone was talking about the fabulous party hosted at your residence. Please accept my humble apologies for missing out on your celebrations.

As you are aware, my mother is suffering from a chronic lung ailment. On the day of the occasion, my mother had to be hospitalized and necessitated immediate medical attention since her health declined due to shortness of breath. Since it was an emergency, I could not inform you beforehand. However, I am planning to host a supper for you at my house next Sunday evening, in your respect, and I can hope to make up for skipping your commemoration.

I am looking forward to meeting you in person to congratulate you. Besides, I also seek your forgiveness for not honouring your invitation.

Yours lovingly,
Justin Green

154 Words

Vocab for task – 4

- Chronic – prolonged
- Ailment – illness
- Beforehand – earlier
- Supper – dinner / evening meal
- Commemoration – tribute / celebration

TASK 5

You want to join a gym. Write a letter to a friend asking them to join you. In your letter Include

- *Why do you want to exercise*
- *What types of exercises you are planning to do*
- *Why do you want your friend to join you*

Write at least 150 words

Dear Daniel,

I am thrilled to inform you that I intend to purchase a gym membership at Planet Fitness on King's Street. I hope you can accompany me to the gym to improve our general fitness.

Since, you know, I am going on a trekking excursion involving six days of excruciating hiking in the Canadian Rockies. Therefore, I must achieve the optimal fitness level required to complete the challenging mountain course. The experts have directed me to perform cardiovascular workouts to improve my stamina and emphasize muscle building. I will be working out on rowing and treadmill equipment. I know that you are also laying the groundwork for the same adventure, therefore, joining the gym will give us the essential vigour for the trekking.

Besides, we will accomplish the tasks effortlessly if we sweat together and motivate each other to push our limits while performing at the gym.

I am eagerly waiting for your response and suggestions.

Best regards,
Justin Green

161 words

Vocab for test – 5

- Excursion – tour
- Excruciating – unbearable
- Optimal – ideal / best
- Vigour – energy / enthusiasm

TASK 6

You drive to work. However, you recently had a problem parking your car at the office. Write a letter to your manager. In your letter

- *describe the problem with the parking*
- *explain how this is affecting you*
- *suggest what should be done about the problem*

Write at least 150 words

Dear Sir,

I am writing this letter to bring to your kind attention that despite having a parking lot in our office building, I cannot park my car at the facility.

Since the security contract of our company expired last month, there are no caretakers at its gates. Our organization has not hired any other service provider, which has led to an increased number of incidents involving vandalism. A few days ago, some troublemakers smashed the rear mirror of my car, which has terrorized me to the core.

I refrain from parking my vehicle at my designated spot, and by paying unnecessary, I prefer to park it in a private space. It has become inconvenient as I oversee the night shift, and I fear for my safety when I walk back alone to the car during the wee hours.

I request you to renew the security contract to avoid unnecessary distress to other employees and me.

I hope you will take the necessary action and resolve the crisis immediately.

Yours sincerely,
Justin Green

173 Words

Vocab for task – 6

- Vandalism – damage / destruction
- troublemaker – person often causing troubles
- Refrain – avoid doing / abstain
- Designated – selected / chosen
- Distress – anguish / misery / pain
- Crisis – crunch / disaster

TASK 7

An English-speaking friend would like to visit your town/city and has written to you to ask for some advice. Write a letter to this friend. In your letter

- *say when the best time to visit your town/city is*
- *tell your friend what the most interesting places are*
- *suggest where they can find cheap accommodation*

Write at least 150 words

Dear Allen,

I am overly thrilled to know that you are planning a trip to my city. You will love visiting Kuala Lumpur as it is a leading tourist destination and an amalgamation of diverse cultures.

Foremost, you must come in March as the weather is moderate and most festivals fall during the springtime. There are numerous tourist hotspots as well as fascinating local attractions, which you can explore.

The city is on the banks of the famous 'Klang' river. You can indulge in various adventurous activities such as rafting, rowing, and scuba diving. There is an incredible hill station nearby known as Genting Highlands, which gives the vantage point to the city's stunning skyline. If you want to shop as natives, you must include in your itinerary 'central market', the traditional shopping complex located in China Town. You can find decent and economical accommodation options nearby the shopping centre, as this area is highly popular with backpackers.

I am excited about meeting you and to show you some stunning places in and around my city.

Yours lovingly,
Justin Green

180 Words

Vocab for task – 7

- Amalgamation – union
- Fascinating – attractive
- Vantage – point of view
- Stunning – eye-catching
- Backpackers – travellers

TASK 8

You are starting a new business and need to build a website. You have a friend who works for an IT company who wants to help you. Write a letter to this friend. In your letter

- *describe your new business*
- *ask your friend to help you build the website*
- *say how you will thank your friend for his/her help*

Write at least 150 words

Dear Daniel,

While writing this letter, I am exhilarated to inform you that I am in the final stages of launching my latest business venture, and I want your help in creating its website.

I am opening a new store that will include all the goods and equipment related to sports and outdoor adventurous activities. I aim to focus on garnering young consumers of the city who are tech-savvy and prefer to purchase on e-commerce platforms. I want to integrate my online and offline business by offering all my catalogue items on both platforms to maximize the customer experience and revenue. Since you have vast experience in leading IT divisions, I hope you will support me in developing the website as per our product requirement.

Besides, for your motivation and as a token of respect for investing your time and efforts, I am willing to offer you a five percent share of my profits generated from online sales.

I am eagerly waiting for your response to guide me through this new venture.

Yours lovingly,
Justin Green

176 Words

Vocab for task -8

- Exhilarated – overjoyed
- Venture – project
- Garnering – gathering
- Integrate – combine / put together

TASK 9

Recently you saw an article in a newspaper/journal about a city/town you know and some of the information in that article was incorrect. Write a letter to the editor regarding this. In your letter, you should tell:

- *how you know about this city/town*
- *what information was incorrect*
- *what the editor should do about this*

Write at least 150 words

Dear Sir,

I want to bring to your kind attention that you have printed a piece of incorrect information in an article covering the origins of Toronto city in the September edition of Wonder Planet magazine.

I have spent most of my childhood in Toronto and lived there for 25 years of my early life before moving to the United States. Since I was born in the city, I was always fascinated by its unique history and culture. I accomplished a Major in the history of Canada from the University of Toronto and have been teaching about it for ten years.

Your article is well-researched and beautifully penned, however, at the beginning of the second paragraph, information regarding the city's name traced to Europeans calling it Taranto is incorrect. As per government records and testimonials of oral history of indigenous people, the area was known as "Tkaranto", meaning "where there are trees in the water."

I request you to amend the article and publish the correct information as it undermines the history of Indigenous people and fellow Canadians.

I hope you will immediately take corrective action and will update your story.

Sincerely,
Justin Green

194 Words

Vocab for task – 9

- Fascinated – getting attracted / mesmerized
- Penned – written / composed
- Testimonials – statements / references
- Indigenous – original / native
- Amend – make changes / revise
- Undermines – weakens / damages
- Corrective – remedial

TASK 10

Write a letter to your manager about your work from last year. Include

- *What you did*
- *What do you think you could improve*
- *A training request*

Write at least 150 words

Dear Sir,

I am writing this letter to bring to your kind attention that we must make drastic modifications to improve our business website to make it more user-friendly for our customers.

Last year, I developed an e-commerce platform for our organization to sell our catalogued products directly to our customers. I was assigned to design the interface for the customers and our employees to operate the website.

Since launching it commercially, we have not upgraded any aspects of it. Due to my limited knowledge of the subject, I could not address various technical concerns and add user-friendly features to our site. I suggest that if we can integrate online payment options on our website, it will be convenient for buyers to make payments, which can yield higher revenues.

To acquire advanced education on this matter, I request your permission to attend a technical workshop, which will broaden the spectrum of my skills required to stay ahead of our competitors.

I am eagerly waiting for your reply and approval of my training request.

Sincerely,
Justin Green

176 Words

Vocab for task -10

- Integrate – combine / put together
- Convenient – suitable
- Yield – produce
- Acquire – gain / get hold of
- Spectrum – range / variety

TASK 11

You recently went on a trip and thought that the tour guide was particularly helpful. Now you would like to show him/ her your appreciation. Write a letter to the manager of the tour company. In your letter

- *describe the tour*
- *explain why you liked the tour guide*
- *say what you would like the manager to do to reward the tour guide*

Write at least 150 words

Dear Sir,

Last week I went on a full-day city tour of Vancouver offered by your organization, which was under the able guidance of Daniel. I want to acknowledge and appreciate his extensive knowledge through this letter.

I just loved the excursion as it covered all the famous attractions. It allowed me to connect with the indigenous traditions as Daniel is well-versed in the history and culture of all the places related to natives.

He encapsulates the audience with his way of telling ancient tales, drawing everyone to him. Since I wanted to write food blogs, Daniel was kind enough to educate me on the culinary habits of indigenous people.

Since I had to leave the tour mid-way due to some urgent reasons, I had no opportunity to show appreciation for his kindness and passion. Thus, I am sending a gift for Daniel along with this letter to show my gratitude.

I hope you will pass my compliments on to Daniel.

Sincerely,
Justin Green

164 Words

Vocab for task – 11

- Excursion – tour
- Indigenous – native
- Natives – locals
- Encapsulates – summarize
- Gratitude – thankfulness

TASK 12

Your friend is about to move into a new house. Write a letter to your friend. In your letter

- *offer to help him/her move*
- *explain how exactly you can help*
- *ask him/her some questions about the new house*

Write at least 150 words

Dear Gordan,

I am overjoyed to congratulate you on shifting to a new home.

Since moving can be an agonising task, I want to extend my assistance required for relocating. I will be delighted to deploy my station wagon to move large household items as it has a spacious boot space, and we can transport most of your stuff.

I possess numerous cardboard boxes and bubble wrap rolls that I will be bringing to safeguard your fragile belongings while transporting them in the car. I will also bring meals for you until you have a functioning kitchen.

I will be obliged if you can divulge some details about your new house regarding the total covered area of the property, its value, and the number of rooms as I am also looking for a new place.

I hope you can give me precious input on my queries. I am available to you round the clock for your moving plans.

Regards,
Justin Green

161 Words

Vocab for task – 12

- Agonising – painful
- Deploy – implement / set up
- Obliged – grateful
- Divulge – reveal

TASK 13

You are planning a vacation and want your friend to go with you. Write a letter to your friend. In your letter, you should tell him/her

- *why do you want to take a vacation*
- *describe your plan*
- *invite him/her to go with you*

Write at least 150 words

Dear Shaun,

I hope this letter finds you in good health. I am thrilled to inform you that I am organizing a retreat to Malaysia, and I want you to join me on this adventure to make it an unforgettable expedition.

Since we graduated, we were unable to celebrate your valedictorian achievement due to the sudden rise of the Corona pandemic and the shutting down of international travel. As the situation has significantly improved, I am thinking of going to Malaysia to celebrate our hard-earned qualifications before we begin our professional careers.

I am planning to visit Kuala Lumpur in the last week of December as it is considered the optimal weather to travel there. The New Year's Eve festivities are celebrated majestically there and are renowned worldwide. We can also explore different areas of the city and visit nearby hill stations. I know that you will enjoy it, therefore, I invite you to accompany me on this memorable voyage.

I am eagerly waiting for your reply and wish to meet you soon.

Love,
Justin Green

176 Words

Vocab for task – 13

- Retreat – move away / holiday
- Expedition – trip
- Valedictorian – scholar
- Optimal – best
- Majestically – magnificently / royally
- Voyage – journey

TASK 14

You are leaving your job and would like to invite your friend to replace you. Write a letter to your friend. In your letter, you should

- *describe the job*
- *explain the reason you are leaving*
- *tell him/her why you would recommend the job to them*

Write at least 150 words

Dear Ray,

I hope my letter finds you in good health and in the best of spirits. I wish to inform you that I am resigning from my current job next month, and I am going to recommend you as the successor to my post.

I have been discharging responsibilities as the chief recruiting officer for 15 years in the computer software department. My duties included searching and appointing young talent directly through campus placements. I was involved in designing training programs to enhance the skills of young entrants to maximize the development of future human resources.

Since I am leaving India permanently to settle abroad, the directors have asked me to endorse a person as my replacement. I reckon that you are highly suitable for this position as you are the most hardworking person in the industry.

This opportunity will allow you to showcase your creativity and talent globally. Moreover, you have the experience to execute duties effectively as demanded by the recruiters.

I hope you will carefully consider my suggestion and reply as soon as possible.

Regards,
Justin Green

181 Words

Vocab for task – 14

- Recruiting – employing
- Entrants – applicants
- Endorse – support / favour
- Execute – perform / implement
- Recruiters – choosers

TASK 15

Write a letter to your manager to request setting up a cafeteria for the staff. In your letter, you should tell:

- **what have you heard about the inconvenience from the staff**
- **how do you feel about it**
- **what suggestions do you have**

Write at least 150 words

Dear Sir,

I am writing this letter to bring to your kind notice that our office has no cafeteria facility, therefore, the staff is facing several inconveniences while having their meals during the day.

Employees have been complaining that they are forced to visit a nearby restaurant to have their meals or snacks. I reckon they are spending most of their break time commuting between the office and the eatery.

I feel that this trivial concern is hurting their morale as well as the productivity of the team. I recommend you to immediately dedicate a space for a coffee machine and other appliances where everyone can sit comfortably during the lunch breaks.

We have an empty lot on the second floor and some extra benches and tables are lying there, which may be utilized to create a cafeteria to provide convenience for our hardworking workforce.

I hope you will consider my request soon to set up the lunchroom.

Yours sincerely,
Justin Green

162 Words

Vocab for task -15

- Trivial – insignificant
- Morale – confidence
- Convenience – ease

TASK 16

Recently you visited a foreign country with a friend. Write a letter to someone, you should tell

- *why you enjoyed the trip*
- *what you are doing now*
- *invite her to visit you*

Write at least 150 words

Dear Jena,

How are you? I hope you are in good health. I am thrilled to inform you that I am back from a magnificent vacation in Thailand.

My escapade was beyond incredible as I enjoyed every day of my stay at the hotel Marriot in Krabi. Since I was with Dan, we were able to accomplish exhilarating activities. We went to Krabi, a beautiful island and enjoyed paragliding and river rafting in the Andaman Sea. Being the food capital of the world, I was delighted to experience traditional Thai and Chinese cuisine there. We ate at several street food stalls and loved the hospitality of the natives.

I have extended my leave period at work by seven more days and have ample leisure time till next Sunday.

I will be extremely delighted if you can join me in my hometown next weekend. I wish to tell you about all the highlights of my journey in detail so that we can plan a future retreat together.

I am eagerly looking forward to your reply and to meeting you.

Yours lovingly,
Justin Green

182 Words

Vocab for task – 16

- Magnificent – stunning / beautiful
- Escapade – adventure / trip
- Exhilarating – thrilling / excited
- Ample – plenty / abundant
- Retreat – holiday / hideaway

TASK 17

Your friend has just moved to a new house. Write a letter to your friend and let him know about the gift that you bought for him/her. In your letter, you should:

- *describe the gift*
- *tell how it will be delivered*
- *explain why you chose it*

Write at least 150 words

Dear David,

I am overjoyed while writing this letter to congratulate you on your new house. I am elated to inform you that I have selected a perfect housewarming present for you.

You will be thrilled to know that the gift is a music system of the Sony brand, which is renowned to deliver incredible sound. I know you will love this gift as you were desperately exploring this specific product in the market.

It was unavailable locally and I had it imported specially from Japan. It will be delivered to you through the courier by next week at your new address. This marvellous audio system consists of two subwoofers and four speakers set for the 'digital sound' effect. It can play all music formats through several modes like compact discs, music cassettes, and Bluetooth.

Since you are a big music buff, I wish to give you something that you may cherish for a long time and utilize in your routine.

I hope you will love my gesture and enjoy playing songs on it.

Yours lovingly,
Justin Green

178 Words

Vocab for task – 17

- Elated – overjoyed / ecstatic
- Incredible – amazing / extraordinary
- Marvellous – magnificent
- Cherish – relish
- Gesture – action

TASK 18

You recently had a job interview which went well but you are still awaiting their decision. Write a letter to the HR manager of the company. In your letter, you should

- *Give the job details*
- *Explain why the interview went well*
- *Ask when you will know their decision*

Write at least 150 words

Dear sir,

I am writing this letter to inquire about the status of the job interview that I had given last Tuesday at the corporation's primary office.

The job opening is for the financial manager at the organization's latest branch located in Toronto. The chief responsibilities included maintaining books, preparing financial budgets, and formulating the fiscal policy of the company's subsidiaries. The contract offered was for full-time employment incorporating a term of 5 years with an option to extend for further 3 years on mutual consent.

The interviewers were extremely convinced by my articulate presentation on the latest accounting principles and my previous experience. I was informed to contact you in case of any query. My current employer expects me to give a 30-day advance notice to change jobs.

I would be grateful if you could inform me about the outcome of the interview so that I can plan accordingly.

I am looking forward to a prompt response.

Yours truly,
Justin Green

162 Words

Vocab for task – 18

- Fiscal – financial
- Subsidiaries - additional
- Incorporating – combining / add in
- Consent – approval
- Articulate – clear
- Prompt – quick / on time

TASK 19

You had dinner with a family friend. Write a letter to your friend to say

- *What you liked about the dinner*
- *Your feelings about their family*
- *Invite your friend and their family to your place*

Write at least 150 words

Dear Daniel,

I am filled with gratitude while writing this letter. I want to express my humble appreciation towards you and your family for hosting the supper.

At dinner, your mother presented all the main course dishes in an extraordinary style that I could not resist tasting them all. I relished everything prepared by your mother and, I can say with utter confidence that she is a culinary expert. I was surprised at the variety of food items, and especially the chicken broth infused with Thai herbs was extremely delicious.

During the dinner, I felt I was around my kin as your parents are openhearted and full of warmth. As a token of my respect and thankfulness, I want to extend an invitation to you and your family to join me at my place for a meal next Sunday and allow me to cater to you.

Once again, I am grateful for the wonderful dining experience, and I wish to return the gesture to you and your family.

Best regards,
Justin Green

172 Words

Vocab for task – 19

- Gratitude – thankfulness
- Supper – evening meal / dinner
- Relish – savour / delight
- Utter – total / sheer
- Culinary – cooking
- Infused – put in / soaked
- Kin – family / relative
- Cater – provide / offer / serve

TASK 20

You stayed over at a friend's house last weekend and think that you left your watch there. In your letter, you should

- *Thank your friend*
- *Describe your watch*
- *Tell them what you want him to do*

Write at least 150 words

Dear Sam,

I want to express my gratitude to you for being a wonderful host. I thoroughly enjoyed the stay at your home, and during good times, I inadvertently forgot my watch at your house.

I remember vividly that I had removed my watch and placed it securely in the cupboard's drawer before going to sleep. However, the next morning when I was getting ready to leave, I forgot to wear it, and I realized my mistake after reaching home. You will certainly recognize the watch as it bears my initials 'J.G.' engraved on the back of the dial and its safety case. The watch is of the Apple brand, and it is white in colour with a black wristband.

Since I have some work in your neighbourhood next Monday, I will collect it from you. Till then, please keep the watch with you.

I want to convey my appreciation for helping me, and I am looking forward to meeting you soon.

Best regards,
Justin Green

166 Words

Vocab for task – 20

- Inadvertently – unintentionally / accidently
- Vividly – clearly
- Engraved – imprinted / carved

TASK 21

You work in an international company and want to request some time off to attend a family event. Write to your manager

- *Ask for time off*
- *Describe the event*
- *Say how you will make up the time missed*

Write at least 150 words

Dear Sir,

I am working as a junior accountant in the finance department of our corporation. I am writing this letter to obtain permission for a leave, starting 1st December till 14th December, for attending my sister's marriage.

I am aware that the time requested is a little more than the usual days authorized by the company's policy for family engagements. However, the wedding is of my younger sibling and is being solemnized in another city. I necessitate more time for arrangements for the events as the marriage involves several rituals to be completed over the period of five days.

I have already compiled the accounts for December and have completed all my work-related commitments imminent for the present month, therefore, my absence will not hinder work at the office. For making up for the additional break, I commit to working double shifts for a week without claiming any overtime bonuses.

I hope you will accede to my request given the special circumstances, and I would be grateful if you may grant me leave.

Yours truly,
Justin Green

180 Words

Vocab for task -21

- Sibling – brother or sister
- Solemnized – honoured / celebrated
- Imminent – pending / looming / approaching
- Hinder – obstruct
- Accede – agree / assent

TASK 22

You just finished a course and borrowed a book from the teacher but could not return it on time. You would like to return the book now. Write to your teacher

- *Describing the book*
- *Saying how helpful the book was*
- *Explaining why you didn't return it before*

Write at least 150 words

Dear sir,

I hope this letter finds you in good health and in high spirits. I want to seek your forgiveness for keeping your book for a period longer than expected.

Before my diploma examinations, I borrowed the latest edition of 'Advance Accounting' authored by D.B. Moore from you. I was able to comprehend broad knowledge of international accounting standards by practising from this book.

The mock tests, along with the chapters, were extremely helpful for preparing for the finals. You will be delighted to know that your kindness to loan me the book has assisted me to secure merit on my accounting examination.

Since the sudden outbreak of the pandemic, my paper was adjourned to March, which caused the unintentional delay in returning your book. I will deliver your book by the next weekend at your residence and will seek an apology in person.

Please pardon me for any inconvenience caused to you because of the inordinate delay.

Yours sincerely,
Justin Green

163 Words

Vocab for task – 22

- Comprehend – understand
- Adjourned – put off / postponed / delayed
- Unintentionally – by accident
- Pardon – forgiveness
- Inordinate – excessive / disproportionate

TASK 23

Write a letter to your landlord to ask about repair work that was not completed successfully.

- *What the problem was*
- *What the repairers did*
- *What do you expect*

Write at least 150 words

Dear Heather,

I am writing this letter to bring to your kind attention that the reparation of the water pipes on the first floor has not been carried out completely, due to which I am facing an acute water shortage.

The constant dripping of the pipeline from the overhead tank has obstructed the flow and pressure of water on the ground floor. Last time, the plumber was able to fix only one of the points of seepage, which improved the supply of water. However, the repair works were not completed.

I hope you will immediately arrange the necessary technician for maintenance as I am struggling to access water for my daily chores. The puddle of water on the roof may also compromise the structure of the building, which may prove to be fatal for all the tenants. This is an issue that must be dealt with without any delay.

I assume you will resolve the matter urgently to relieve me from further inconvenience.

Yours truly,
Justin Green

167 Words

Vocab for task – 23

- Reparation – repair work / amendment
- Acute – severe / sharp
- Dripping – soaked
- Seepage – leakage
- Chores – everyday jobs
- Puddle – lake / pond
- Fata l- deadly

TASK 24

Write a letter to a colleague asking for assistance in setting up equipment for an upcoming presentation of yours. Include

- *What the presentation is about*
- *The equipment needed*
- *Ask for assistance in setting it up*

Write at least 150 words

Dear Johnson,

I am writing this letter to seek your cooperation in arranging the essential set-up for my presentation on the annual financial budget of the company next Friday.

The scope of my project is the marketing budgets of our organization for the next economic year. I will be covering the cost of acquisition of customers incurred through various modes of advertisements. I am preparing to showcase all the information in a multimedia format to capture the attention and make it easier for the audience to comprehend at a single glance.

I require your assistance to install a projector and a white screen in the conference room to deliver an audio-visual demonstration. I hope you may aid me in positioning the items one day before the event, it will allow me to have ample time to get familiar with the apparatus. Since the room is congested, please install the wires along the roof to prevent any inconvenience during the meeting.

I shall be indebted to you if you can provide me with your expertise in arranging the system for presentation.

Yours truly,
Justin Green

184 Words

Vocab for task – 24

- Incurred – suffered / acquired
- Congested – packed full / crowded
- Indebted – thankful / grateful

TASK 25

Write a letter to a foreign friend who has asked if they can stay with you when visiting your country. Include

- *Why you do not have time to host them*
- *An alternate date*
- *Recommendations for what to do*

Write at least 150 words

Dear Ethan,

How are you? I want to seek your apology for not being able to provide accommodation for you during the visit.

The calendar of my final examinations is coinciding with your travel plans. Since my university is in another province, I must travel there for writing exams, therefore, I will not be available to host you. I will be overjoyed if you have the flexibility to postpone your arrival till 24th December as my annuals will be concluded by then. I will have spare time between semesters to host you and spend time with you.

I reckon you should verify with your airlines if they can reschedule your flights for a later date. However, if you are unable to amend your itinerary, I will arrange substitute accommodation at my friend's house. Shaun will be delighted to assist you in my absence.

I am keenly waiting to meet you soon and hope you will reorganize your trip accordingly.

Your friend,
Justin Green

163 Words

Vocab for task – 25

- Coinciding – overlapping / corresponding
- Amend – make changes
- Substitute – alternative / additional

TASK 26

You recently took a trip to another city, and you had the plan to visit your friend who is living there. However, you couldn't see him/her. Write a letter to your friend, and say

- *Apologize for not being able to meet*
- *Give your reasons*
- *Suggest how you can meet some other time*

Write at least 150 words

Dear Ellen,

I hope this letter will find you in good health and high spirits. I am writing to seek your forgiveness for not meeting you as per my commitment.

Since my visit to your city was scheduled for three days, I reserved the second day exclusively for our reunion. However, my mother met with an accident and was hospitalized, necessitating immediate medical attention. I had to cut short my vacation and went back to my hometown on the initial day itself. I could not inform you beforehand as it was unforeseen, and I had to leave immediately. Now she is recovering at home and is in better condition.

Nevertheless, I have a business summit next Sunday on the outskirts of your town. I will be elated if you could join me for dinner at my hotel, which will grant me an opportunity to absolve myself.

I hope you will accept my humble apology and spare some time from your busy routine to meet me.

Your friend,
Justin Green

169 Words

Vocab for task -26

- Unforeseen – unexpected
- Outskirts – outer edge / county area
- Elated – overjoyed
- Absolve – forgive / excuse

TASK 27

You have purchased a product on a website and received a different product. Write a letter to the company. In your letter

- *Describe the product you ordered*
- *Explain why you aren't satisfied with the product you received*
- *Let them know what actions you expect them to take*

Write at least 150 words

Dear Sir,

I am a loyal consumer of your e-commerce portal and have purchased numerous items. Recently on 1st January, I purchased a baby stroller of the Chicco brand, but I was delivered the incorrect item.

I specifically ordered the stroller for the ages 3 and above in the red colour. The cost of the product is CAD 404, and its product identification number is 'C-1121'. I received an item that seems to be of inferior quality and belongs to a different brand name and colour. As per the product description, it is meant for infants only, therefore, not suitable for my requirements.

I have never faced such an issue with your immaculate delivery system, but this time I want a replacement. Furthermore, please ensure I am not charged any incidental expenses for shipping and picking up items as it was not my fault.

I assume you will act promptly to rectify the error by supplying me with the appropriate article.

Yours sincerely,
Justin Green

165 Words

Vocab for task – 27

- infant – new-born
- Immaculate – flawless / perfect
- Incidental – supplementary / additional
- Promptly – quickly / swiftly
- Rectify – mend / resolve

TASK 28

Write a letter to your friend inviting him/her to a music concert. Please say

- *Where and when does the concert start*
- *What type of music will be played there*
- *Why do you think your friend will enjoy it*

Write at least 150 words

Dear Nathan,

How are you? I hope you are safe. I am thrilled to inform you that the greatest music concert in the country is slated to occur in my city and hope we can attend it together.

The event is organized on New Year's Eve at George Bell Arena located at Union Station. It will commence at 9 p.m. and will conclude at 1 a.m., therefore, we will celebrate the new year at the concert among other music buffs.

The leading attraction is the performance by legendary pop icon 'Akon', and it will also feature our favourite musician, 'David Guetta', alongside him. Throughout the show, artists will be singing American pop music. I reckon besides the performances; you will appreciate the culinary and historical aspects of the event.

You will be delighted to know that the music festival will also include an extensive presentation of memorabilia associated with pop culture. Furthermore, several American delicacies are included in the buffet that will be served at the venue.

I am eagerly waiting for your response, and I am excited to attend this festival with you.

Lovingly,
Justin Green

187 Words

Vocab for task -28

- Slated – scheduled
- Music buff – people who love music
- Culinary – related to food / cooking
- Delicacies – treats / luxury items
- Memorabilia – souvenir / collectible

TASK 29

You have just finished your master's degree and need to leave your current part-time job to search for full-time employment. Write a letter to your current employer. In your letter:

- *explain why you will not be able to pursue a full-time job in his/her company*
- *say why you've enjoyed working for him/her*
- *tell him/her how much longer you will continue to work for him/her*

Write at least 150 words

Dear Sir,

I am writing this letter to resign from my part-time job as a junior accountant.

I was pursuing my master's degree in Advanced Accounting, which restricted me to only perform on weekends. Since I have accomplished my studies, I desire to work full-time. I would enjoy continuing work in this corporation, however, there is no vacant position available for a full-time employee in the foreseeable future.

I want to express my gratitude to you for granting me the opportunity to be employed along with an experienced accountant like yourself. Working for you was a delightful journey. I acquired paramount knowledge of accounting principles and life skills, and you taught everything with extraordinary patience. I will be able to officiate my duties until the 1st of the next month. This letter is my intent to serve the two-week notice period mandatory to leave the job.

I am confident that I can put you as my reference for my prospective employers and look forward to hearing from you.

Yours truly,
Justin Green

172 Words

Vocab for task – 29

- Foreseeable – predictable / probable
- Paramount – supreme / utmost
- Extraordinary – remarkable / astonishing
- Mandatory – compulsory

TASK 30

During a recent plane journey, you sat next to a businessman who owns a chain of restaurants. You talked to him and suggested that you should contact him about a possible job in one of his restaurants.

- *remind him when and where you met*
- *tell him what kind of job you are interested in*
- *say why you think you would be suitable for the job*

Write at least 150 words

Dear Sir,

I am writing this letter about a potential employment opportunity offered by you.

I hope you may remember me from the aeroplane journey from Bangkok to New York in December. We were engrossed in an engaging conversation on various topics of economics during the flight's duration.

After learning about my educational and work antecedents, you instructed me to contact you for a prospective job in your hospitality company. Presently, I am working as a junior pastry chef for Marriot, Krabi. I have accomplished graduation in baking skills from the London School of Culinary Arts. I am looking forward to being employed in the relevant sector as a senior chef to exhibit my capabilities with more freedom.

I am aware your restaurants are expanding to include pastry and cake sections in their menu. I can assist you with designing a suitable menu and a course of action necessary to attract consumers to expand the business through my vast experience in this field.

I want to express gratitude for your kindness and assume you will reply promptly.

Yours sincerely,
Justin Green

181 Words

Vocab for task – 30

- Engrossed – occupied
- Antecedents – experiences
- Prospective – potential / probable
- Promptly – quickly / swifty

TASK 31

A large Company in your area has decided to spend a certain amount of money, either to sponsor a local children's sports team for two years or to pay for two open-air concerts. It has asked for feedback from the general public.

- **describe the *benefits of sponsoring the sports team***
- ***summarise the benefits of paying for the concerts***
- ***say how you think the company should spend the money***

Write at least 150 words

Dear Sir,

I am a resident of the Bana Hills neighbourhood, and I would like to express my gratitude to your organization for offering to invest a generous amount for the development and entertainment of our children.

The kid's football team of our local club is playing amazingly at the junior level, and they have qualified to participate in the international junior world championship to be held next month in Japan. Your monetary support to the team for two years will encourage young players to perform incredibly in the future without worrying about expenses associated with the sport. Your kind gesture will contribute to inculcating the sporting culture in the youth of this area. It will inspire others to partake in the games and will help in preventing juvenile delinquency.

Providing funds for concerts will help in promoting the local artists and culture. It will be a tremendous source of amusement for the vicinity as well.

I urge you to weigh both options pragmatically, but I reckon we ought to spend on the local sports team as it will have positive long-term effects on the future of our young generation.

Yours truly,
Justin Green

194 Words

Vocab for task - 31

- Monetary – financial
- Incredibly – extremely
- Inculcating – instilling / infusing
- Partake – participate
- Juvenile – young
- Delinquency – criminal behaviour
- Amusement – enjoyment
- Vicinity – surrounding area / neighbourhood
- Urge – insist
- Pragmatically – sensibly / rationally

TASK 32

You work at home and have a problem with a piece of equipment that you use for your job. Write a letter to the shop or company which supplied the equipment. In your letter

- *Describe the problem with your equipment*
- *Explain how this problem is affecting your work*
- *Say what you want the shop or company to do*

Write at least 150 words

Dear Sir,

Recently on 21st December, I purchased a laptop of the HP brand bearing model no. 2121 from your exclusive shop located at Dufferin Mall and I am facing numerous issues with it.

Since the beginning, I was facing the problem of the computer system's base getting overheated. I reported the issue to your customer services several times, but the representatives suggested I should wait for a few days as it is a common problem with new machines. In every correspondence, they assured me the trouble would disappear after some time.

However, last night, I was working on my project, and the equipment software crashed abruptly, and the laptop stopped functioning. I am a data analyst, so the computer is vital to accomplish my work. I am suffering, and my assignment is getting delayed because of the malfunctioning of your product.

I request you to replace my laptop within a week as it is covered by the guarantee period. Besides, I require a substitute laptop meanwhile to officiate responsibilities.

I presume you will act promptly to resolve my grievance.

Yours truly,
Justin Green

184 Words

Vocab for task - 32

- Correspondence – connection
- Abruptly – suddenly
- Malfunctioning – faulty / failing / out of order
- Substitute – alternative / extra
- Presume – assume / think
- Resolve – solve
- Grievance – complaint

TASK 33

Write a letter to the owner regarding loud noise coming out of their restaurant which is located near to your house. In your letter, you should

- *state the problem*
- *tell why you are disturbed*
- *suggest how to solve the problem*

Write at least 150 words

Dear Sir,

I wanted to bring to your kind notice that I am facing extreme inconvenience due to noise from loud music emanating out of your establishment in the wee hours.

My house is just across the street from your restaurant. Therefore, I am unable to sleep properly due to the high pitch of the music. In the past, I have made numerous requests to your manager to lower the sound, however, my grievances have fallen on deaf ears as my complaint is still unresolved.

Since I am a student at the University, I am unable to focus on my studies during the night, which has resulted in poor academic performance in the last semester. Furthermore, continuous noise exposure is depriving me of healthy sleep.

I request you to restrict the music volume in the late hours to reasonable levels to avoid any nuisance to me and others.

I am hoping that you will act promptly to take measures to resolve the matter.

Yours truly,
Justin Green

167 Words

Vocab for task - 33

- Emanating – arising / originating
- Wee hours – early morning hours
- High-pitch – sharp
- Grievances – complaints
- Depriving – denying
- Nuisance – annoyance / irritation

TASK 34

You borrowed something from your friend, later it got damaged. Write a letter to your friend. In your letter, you should

- *apologies about the issue*
- *tell how it got damaged*
- *say you are going to fix this issue*

Write at least 150 words

Dear David,

I hope this letter will find you in good health and high spirits.

I want you to accept my humble apologies for accidentally damaging the display screen of your laptop. I will be unable to return it this week as it requires some restoration work.

While I was going home after successfully submitting my project, the laptop bag slipped from my hands and fell on the floor. Consequently, the screen has stopped functioning due to the impact of the drop. I immediately went to the authorized service bureau of the manufacturer to get it repaired.

The engineer assessed the extent of damage caused to the machine and assured me that there are no signs of significant harm to its core modules. However, the display unit of the laptop will be replaced to make it operational, which may take up to seven days. I will return the laptop after it gets functional, and I will bear all the incidental expenses incurred during the process.

Please forgive me for causing you unintentional inconvenience.

Yours truly,
Justin Green

177 Words

Vocab for task – 34

- Restoration – rebuilding / re-establishment
- Bureau – department / agency
- Core – centre
- Modules – units / segments / sections
- Incurred – suffered / sustained
- Unintentional – accidental / unintended

TASK 35

Your landlord is asking to increase the rent. Write a letter to him. In your letter, you should tell

- *why do you think the rent shouldn't be increased*
- *how the increase in rent will affect you*
- *what you will do if it is increased*

Write at least 150 words

Dear Nathan,

Today, I received your announcement regarding the increase in the monthly rent of the shop for the next quarter. However, I regret to inform you that I will not be in a position to pay the enhanced amount since it will exert an unnecessary burden on my pocket.

During the testing times of the pandemic, when businesses are struggling due to diminishing customers and falling sales, the market rents are decreasing as the economy is in recession. Last week a similar commercial property in our neighbourhood is leased out at a lower amount than I am currently paying to you.

If you do not wish to roll back your decision, I will be forced to terminate our agreement through legal recourse. Therefore, this letter must be regarded as the mandatory four-week notice necessitated by the contract to vacate the premises.

I am hopeful we can continue our relationship on good terms, and that you will revoke your unjust demand.

Yours truly,
Justin Green

165 Words

Vocab for task – 35

- Enhanced – improved
- Recession – decline / slump
- Terminate – finish
- Recourse – way out / remedy
- mandatory – compulsory
- vacate – leave
- revoke – cancel / withdraw
- unjust - unfair

TASK 36

You are planning a 2-day work training outside your city next month. Write a letter to the manager of the hotel regarding accommodation arrangements for your visit. In your letter, you should tell

- *introduce yourself and your company*
- *ask about the availability of their rooms*
- *tell him/her your every arrangement and needs*

Write at least 150 words

Dear Sir,

I am Justin Green, Chief manager of Xyz Limited. Our company is the pioneer in transformer manufacturing and overhauling, which have its headquarters in Toronto since 1910.

Our establishment regularly organizes various training programs for our esteemed staff. Therefore, we always look forward to exploring opportunities to establish partnerships with hotels to cater to our conventions. We are planning a two-day skill workshop in the beautiful city of Niagara.

Our demand is for thirty rooms, which must be inclusive of three meals to accommodate our employees. We request you to divulge the details regarding the prices and availability of rooms between the dates 22nd June to 24th June. We necessitate a conference hall, spacious enough for a gathering of forty people and an exclusive dining area.

It will be of great assistance if you will arrange a projector and an audio system for presentations. The sitting layout must be arranged by adhering to the rules and regulations of social distancing.

I am hoping to hear from you promptly with all the answers and a competitive quotation.

Yours truly,
Justin Green

182 Words

vocab for task - 36

- pioneer – forerunner / lead the way
- overhauling – repairing
- esteemed – valued
- cater – serve / offer / provide
- conventions – meetings / conferences
- divulge – reveal / tell / disclose
- necessitate – require
- adhering – sticking / holding

TASK 37

You are planning a vacation and want your friend to go with you. Write a letter to your friend. In your letter, you should

- *tell him/her why you want to take a vacation*
- *describe your plan*
- *invite him/her to go with you*

Write at least 150 words

Dear Amie,

I am elated to inform you that I am arranging an escapade to Aruba for both of us in June to celebrate our graduation ceremony.

I reckon visiting Aruba will be a great way to commemorate our long and difficult academic journey. We can spend our hard-earned leisure time performing beach adventures, and it will be a great escape from Toronto's chilling winters.

I have researched extensively to discover an extremely economical flight to the destination on 12th March, and after spending 10 days there, we will return on the 22nd. Our stay will be at 'The Beach Resort', a luxury five-star hotel with a private beach. I have uncovered an amazing deal, which includes breakfast at no extra cost. I intend to explore all the local sights like the famous church, the old town, and the night market for its shopping experience.

I will be overjoyed if you join me on this dream vacation. I am keenly waiting for your suggestions and reply.

Yours truly,
Justin Green

170 Words

vocab for task – 37

- elated – excited / overjoyed
- escapade – adventure
- commemorate – honour / celebrate
- keenly – eagerly

TASK 38

You recently received an invitation to a three-day training program which should benefit you and your company. Write a letter to your manager and say

- *Ask to attend the program*
- *Describe the program*
- *Explain how the program will benefit the company*

Write at least 150 words

Dear Sir,

I am pleased to inform you that I have been invited to a training program commencing on 10th July. It is being conducted by the International Trade Organisation in Toronto on the recent amendments to the 'Copyrights and Patent Laws'.

I necessitate your authorization to attend this three-day seminar. Therefore, I will be unable to attend the office. The convention will primarily focus on imparting knowledge of the latest trends in international law. Leading professionals will deliver significant lectures regarding the process of registration of patents and copyrights.

This will assist us in enhancing the quality of our services and keeping our corporation ahead of our competitors. It is a momentous prospect for our organization to establish connections and forge relationships with other firms at the international level to expand our footprint. Additionally, it is pertinent for me to keep abreast with the latest information to address appropriately to our client's needs.

I hope to hear from you soon regarding sanctioning my leave to join the conference.

Yours truly,
Justin Green

173 Words

vocab for task – 38

- amendments – changes
- imparting – teaching
- momentous – significant / crucial
- prospect – outlook / chance
- forge – build
- footprint – trail / impression
- pertinent – relevant / appropriate
- abreast – level / side by side
- sanctioning – approving / authorising

TASK 39

You are currently attending a course which is not the same as per the description in the admission brochure. Write a letter to the headmaster. In your letter

- *state which course you are enrolled in*
- *provide details about the noted differences*
- *suggest what actions would you like him to take*

Write at least 150 words

Dear Sir,

I am a student of the Law faculty department in our university's online school of learning. I am pursuing a two-year diploma in 'Patents and Copyrights Law' for the ongoing session.

I am disheartened to bring to your kind notice that the subject of 'Conventions of the United Nations on International Trade' has been omitted in our first semester. This has been substituted by the 'Law on International Patents' without any prior intimation to us. I reckon most of the students were fervent to study conventions since it is the foundation for all the branches of international and domestic law. According to the official handbook covering the scope of the diploma, we were supposed to have classes on conventions before any other subject.

I would request you to immediately start the lectures on conventions, as per the chronology of the admission prospectus, for a better understanding of the course.

I hope you will take prompt action to avoid any inconvenience to students.

Yours truly,
Justin Green

168 Words

vocab for task – 39

- disheartened – discouraged
- omitted – excluded
- substituted – replaced / swapped
- intimation – suggestion / warning
- fervent – passionate / keen
- prospectus – brochure
- chronology – sequential / sequence of events

TASK 40

Your local council is planning to hold an election to choose members from the society but there are no young people on the council, and you think that the council needs young people's views. You are thinking of standing for election. Write a letter to the head of the council. In your letter

- *state why you want to be elected*
- *mention why you think you would be a good candidate*
- *describe your qualities, skills, experience, and interests, if any*

Write at least 150 words

Dear Sir,

I am a young professional who is a resident of your local council limits and practicing law within its jurisdiction. I humbly express my yearning to participate in the upcoming elections for council members to represent the youth of our area.

For the last three years, I have been attending all the meetings of the senate. I have realized that the elected body has no person to resonate with and raise the issues faced by youngsters in our community.

I reckon that particularly young people in our city can relate to me, being a younger candidate, who can understand their hardships and have empathy with them. I have come across shocking statistics regarding our district that most of the youth is unemployed, which has surged the involvement of adolescents in criminal activities.

My field of expertise is criminal law, and I particularly deal with incidents of juvenile delinquency. My experiences in psychology and law will be beneficial to eradicate this pressing issue.

I hope I can become the face and voice of young voters and can work toward their welfare.

Yours truly,
Justin Green

186 Words

vocab for task – 40

- yearning – desire
- senate – governing body
- resonate – reverberate / appeal
- hardships – adversity / sufferings
- empathy – understanding / sympathy / compassion
- surged – risen / swelled
- adolescents – youngsters
- juvenile – young age
- delinquency – criminal behaviour
- eradicate – eliminate / remove

TASK 41

One of your friends is coming back from abroad. But you are held up due to some engagements and are unable to go and receive him at the airport. Write him a letter. In your letter

- *apologize for not being able to come*
- *tell him the reason*
- *suggest him an alternative plan and talk about it*

Write at least 150 words

Dear Daniel,

I am elated that you are finally coming back home after five years of sabbatical. I am writing to seek your forgiveness since I will be unable to meet you at the airport on Monday.

As you are aware, my grandmother is not keeping well for a long time. Yesterday, she had to be hospitalized for due care as her health deteriorated further. I am extremely apologetic for not following the schedule as I will be out of town to visit her next week.

I have made substitute arrangements for you to reach home comfortably and safely. My friend Nathan has generously agreed to pick you up from the airport in his conveyance and will accompany you to your destination. Please suggest any amendments that you want in the new plan.

I hope you will understand my position and I promise to see you the day I return from my hometown.

Yours truly,
Justin Green

157 Words

vocab for task – 41

- elated – excited
- sabbatical – holiday / vacation
- forgiveness- pity / mercy / pardon
- deteriorated – worsened / faded
- apologetic – feeling sorry / remorseful
- conveyance – transport
- amendments – revisions / changes

TASK 42

You stayed in a hotel for some days in an overseas country. You have forgotten some things in the hotel room after checkout. Write a letter to the hotel manager. In your letter

- *inform them about your stay*
- *describe the things that you have forgotten there*
- *state what you want them to do now*

Write at least 150 words

Dear Sir,

I stayed in your hotel Prime International located on Palm Street, California and I checked out on 22nd December from room number 222. I want to bring to your kind attention that I have inadvertently left my Rolex watch and some documents in the room's safe.

The watch is of gold colour vide serial number RLX 3199, and it is easily recognizable as my name's initials are engraved on the backside of the dial as 'J.G.'. The documents are in a red folder bearing my name. I remember vividly that I securely placed my watch and the file in the safe and forgot to collect them while checking out.

I will be exceedingly obliged if you can arrange to ship the items to my official address, i.e., c/o Justin Green, 3 Carlton Street, Suite 9999, Toronto ON M5B 1J3. Moreover, I will bear all the charges and would like you to disclose your bank account details in order to pay for the expenses in advance.

I want to express my gratitude and seek your forgiveness for the inconvenience caused to you.

Yours truly,
Justin Green

187 Words

vocab for task – 42

- inadvertently – unintentionally / by mistake
- engraved – embossed / inscribed / imprinted
- vividly- clearly
- exceedingly – remarkably / extremely
- obliged – grateful

TASK 43

Your friend had planned for you to see a movie together, but you cannot join him now. You have found another friend who can go instead of you. Write a letter to your friend. In your letter

- *Explain why you cannot go anymore*
- *Say who can go instead*
- *Say why this person is a good person to go with*

Write at least 150 words

Dear Daniel,

I am extremely thrilled to watch the upcoming movie 'The grown-ups' by Adam Sandler with you. However, I will not be able to join you at the weekend as I ought to visit my hometown.

Since you are aware that my grandmother was not keeping well, yesterday she had to be hospitalized under extensive care as her health deteriorated rapidly. I must go to take care of her under the given circumstances.

Nevertheless, my friend Nathan has generously agreed to accompany you to the theatre. I reckon you will enjoy his company as much as I enjoy yours, as he is also a huge movie buff just like you and is an ardent fan of Adam Sandler's movie series. I hope you will forgive me for the sudden schedule change and understand my situation.

I am certain that you will take pleasure in watching the picture with Nathan. Maybe next time we all can arrange to watch a movie together.

Lovingly,
Justin Green

165 Words

vocab for task – 43

- deteriorated – worsened
- movie buff – someone who loves watching movies
- ardent – passionate

TASK 44

You are not satisfied with the changing room in the sports centre that you visit. Write a letter to the manager of this sports centre. In your letter, explain

- *what the problem is*
- *how you feel about the problem*
- *what steps do you want the manager to take*

Write at least 150 words

Dear Sir,

I want to bring to your kind notice that last month the water pipes in the changing room were busted, due to which, I am facing extreme inconvenience while using the facility.

The washrooms of the changing room have become obsolete, as they are always damp due to the constant leakage of water. It has become unfeasible to change clothes before and after the workout. The accumulation of water inside the lockers has obliterated my squash equipment stored inside the cabinet.

Furthermore, other members are also being affected by it. The resentment among the users is growing with every passing day by looking at the appalling state of our prestigious sports centre. In the past, I have raised this issue on multiple occasions with the maintenance department, however, they have failed to carry out necessary repairs without assigning any reasonable reason.

I hope you will take corrective action by hiring a professional to replace the damaged pipes without any further ado.

OR

I presume you will take prompt action by hiring a professional to replace the damaged pipes.

Yours truly,
Justin Green

163 Words

vocab for task – 44

- busted – spoiled / ruined
- obsolete – outdated
- damp – wet / humid
- unfeasible – not possible
- obliterated – destroyed
- resentment – anger
- appalling – terrible
- prestigious – impressive
- ado – argument / objection

TASK 45

A local college is having an international day. You want to speak about your country to students from different cultures.

- *tell about topics you are going to talk about*
- *explain why those topics would be interesting for students*
- *ask about the arrangements you need for the talk*

Write at least 150 words

Dear Madam,

I will be pleased to share about my home country, South Africa, on the occasion of International Day celebrations at your college.

I will cover one of the rudiments of African culture, i.e., unity in diversity, at the seminar. I reckon that different communities migrating to Africa have co-existed harmoniously. Similarly, the foundation of Canada remains strong in accepting immigrants with open arms from around the globe. I would like to have an interactive session with the audience on drawing similarities between the life and teachings of Nelson Mandela and the 'worldview' of the indigenous population of Canada.

These topics will kindle plenty of interest among the students, as most of them are new immigrants to our society. Being a settler in this country, I can resonate with their struggles and can assist them in clearing doubts regarding immigration from a legal perspective.

For the presentation, I do not necessitate a complex arrangement. I only require a microphone and projector screen to communicate with the listeners.

I am eagerly waiting for your response and decision.

Yours truly,
Justin Green

181 Words

vocab for task – 45

- rudiments – basics / fundamentals / essentials
- diversity – variety
- harmoniously – agreeably / cordially
- indigenous – native
- kindle – spark
- resonate – appeal
- perspective – view / outlook

TASK 46

Your child is going away on a school trip for three days to another country. The head teacher wants some parents to join the trip and you would like to go.

- *say why would you like to go*
- *suggest what you could do to help during the trip*
- *Ask some more questions about the trip*

Write at least 150 words

Dear Sir,

I will be extremely obliged to share the responsibility as one of the companions for the school's field excursion to Thailand.

Since Thailand is my home country, it will be an amazing occasion for me to accompany students and introduce them to the diverse culture of my community. I have ample experience of travelling extensively in Thailand, and it is always helpful if someone in the group is familiar with the native language of the place. I am a doctor, and I can assist with any medical emergencies during our stay.

I will be grateful if you may provide the name and address of the accommodations where we are slated to stay. Additionally, a list of places that we will be covering during our journey and the cost of the tour to be paid by me.

I am waiting for your prompt reply, and I hope I will be granted the opportunity to join and serve the group.

Yours truly,
Justin Green

164 Words

vocab for task – 46

- obliged – grateful
- companion – friend
- excursion – trip
- extensively – widely
- native – local / indigenous / original
- slated – scheduled / lined up
- grateful – thankful

TASK 47

You live in a room in college which you share with another student. However, there are many problems with this arrangement, and you find it very difficult to work. Write a letter to the accommodation officer at the college. In your letter

- *describe the situation*

- *explain your problems and why it is difficult to work*

- *say what kind of accommodation you would prefer*

Write at least 150 words

Dear Sir,

I am a research scholar at the 'School of Law' and, I have been assigned room number 202 of the 'Lincon hostel' on a sharing basis. I want to bring up an issue regarding my situation of accommodation to your kind notice.

I have been staying in this dormitory for the last six months with a sophomore-year student from the Arts college. He is a budding musician who requires to practise his vocals every day. It becomes impossible for me to focus on my studies while he performs his routine. These days I am writing a thesis with my co-author, which necessitates a peaceful environment for research. There is only one study desk in the room, therefore, we both struggle to study properly as per our schedules. I was forced to accede to this arrangement due to the unavailability of rooms at the beginning of the semester.

Since all doctorate students are entitled to individual accommodation as per university rules, I request you to assign a single occupancy room to me accordingly.

I expect a prompt reply and an appropriate solution to my problem.

Sincerely,
Justin Green

189 Words

vocab for task -47

- dormitory – hall residence / student house
- sophomore-year – second year
- budding – growing / potential
- thesis – theory
- accede – agree
- entitled – eligible

TASK 48

You are applying for a job in an international company. You would like to ask your previous employer to write a reference letter for you. Write a letter to your previous manager. In your letter

- *remind your manager of the job you previously held in the company*
- *tell him/her what position you are applying for and why you want it*
- *ask him/her to provide you with a reference letter*

Write at least 150 words

Dear Sir,

I worked with your organization as an assistant manager from the years 2017 to 2019. I was associated with the marketing team in the retail department and was under your direct supervision.

I would be glad to tell you that your knowledge and principles have always acted as a guiding star throughout my career's landscape. I am planning to apply for the position of creative advertisement director for Amazon, which is a leading multi-national e-commerce group. Since the dawn of my career, I have always aspired to work in the field of media. Therefore, the prospective opportunity grants me the to explore and enhance my creative abilities.

I would be extremely grateful if you could write me a reference letter recommending me for the new job opening on the company's letterhead. It must entail information regarding my job position at your corporation, its accompanying responsibilities, and your opinion regarding my projects.

I am eagerly waiting for your response and reference letter.

Sincerely,
Justin Green

166 Words

vocab for task – 48

- associated – linked
- landscape – scenery
- dawn – start
- aspired – wished / hoped
- prospective – likely / potential
- entail – imply / demand
- grants – funds / donations / awards
- accompanying – additional / supplementary

TASK 49

You own an old item that you think is valuable and would like to sell. Write a letter to the owner of an antique shop. In your letter

- *explain how you found the shop*

- *describe the item that you would like to sell*

- *say how much you would like to sell the item for*

Write at least 150 words

Dear Rick,

I am an ardent follower of your extremely admired television series The Pawn Stars and found your shop through it. I am thrilled to inform you about a valuable necklace that I wish to sell.

It belongs to my great-grandfather, who was a member of the Royal British Army. The story of this necklace is captivating. Since he was leading a unit at the 'North-African' front during the second world war, their division faced great resistance from the local tribes of Libya. He pacified the natives through his diplomatic strategies and inked a treaty for their support against Axis forces.

This necklace was presented to him by the leader of the tribe as a symbol of peace and appreciation. It is pure gold and hand-made by local artisans. It carries artwork that portrays my grandfather shaking hands with the tribe's chief, hinting a peaceful, reciprocal relationship. I am willing to part with this piece of history for $40,000, which is a fair amount considering its cultural and political significance.

I am attaching some pictures of the necklace for your kind perusal and waiting eagerly for your response.

Sincerely,
Justin Green

192 Words

Vocab for task – 49

- ardent – dedicated
- admired – accepted
- captivating – mesmerizing / attractive
- pacified – calmed / soothed
- inked – written
- artisans – artists / craft or skilled workers
- portrays – depicts
- reciprocal – mutual
- perusal – survey / review

TASK 50

You work in an office and have recently been experiencing a health problem. You think that the problem started because of the working conditions in the office. Write a letter to your manager. In your letter

- *describe the health problem*
- *explain why you think it was caused by conditions in the office*
- *suggest what the manager should do to improve the working conditions in the office*

Write at least 150 words

Dear Sir,

I am an assistant manager in the legal department. Recently, I was diagnosed with asthma and enlargement of the lungs due to constant exposure to dusty and damp conditions.

The legal wing is in the basement of our organization, therefore, there are very few windows, and the ventilation is inadequate. Since there are thousands of case files stored, these have been accumulating dust and microorganisms for ages. To worsen the situation, some water pipes are leaking, which contributes to humid conditions.

My doctor has concluded that prolonged exposure to the old dust-laden files and humid environment has caused my body's allergic reactions. This is evident from other employees who are suffering from mild symptoms of early lung diseases as well.

I reckon that we must install air purifiers immediately to improve the quality of the air. For long-term solutions, we must endeavour to digitalize our records, which will improve the working conditions.

I hope you will initiate immediate action for the welfare of the workers. Sincerely,

Justin Green

170 Words

Vocab for task – 50

- diagnosed – identified
- enlargement – swelling
- damp – wet / humid
- inadequate – not sufficient
- accumulating – gathering
- prolonged – extended
- exposure – contact
- dust-laden – full of dust
- symptoms – warning signs
- endeavour – effort / attempt
- digitalize – make a transformation with technology

INSTRUCTIONS FOR WRITING 8 BAND ESSAYS

HOW TO USE THIS BOOK

The following instructions are general guidelines for writing an Essay. If you follow the rules provided in the book, you will be capable of successfully writing an impactful essay for IELTS. I request you to carefully read all the instructions multiple times before you start preparing for your examination. The below-mentioned rules will help you write an essay according to the needs of the question.

Once you understand the instructions, you can go through the solved essays for better understanding. I recommend that after reading the instructions, you must attempt one or two questions given in the book without reading the solution. Thereafter, you can compare your answer/s with the provided answer/s in the book to evaluate your performance.

1. FORMAT

A. Parts Of an Essay

The essay has four or five parts. You must carefully read the question and identify the number of questions asked. After identifying different parts of the question, you must answer every part, in the following manner described in the following tables.

Type of Question	Number of Parts	How to Answer (Opinions Required by Question)
To what extent do you agree or disagree with this statement?	This is only 1-part question	You can either say Yes and write agree or can write why you disagree, or decide why you agree/disagree equally, which is following a neutral approach
Discuss both views and give your own opinion. (If both views are asked, you must present both views equally, i.e. length of both paragraphs must be similar)	This is a 3-part question - discuss both views as stated and need to give your opinion	Yes, present your opinion, it may be one of the views or a combination of both.

Why is this so? Give reasons for this and solutions?	This is a 3-part question	A position is presented on why this is so, the reasons for this issue and solutions to solve the issue.
Do the disadvantages of Technology outweigh the advantages?	This is a 2-part question	Yes, you must clearly say if there are more advantages or more disadvantages.
Why is this so? What effect does it have on the individual and society?	This is a 3-part question	Yes, you must give reasons for the statement and then present the effect it has on 1) the individual and 2) society.

Things to remember:

The Essay must include

1. Introduction
2. Body Paragraphs
3. Conclusion

- Once you have identified the type and parts of the question, you must present your opinion.
- You must answer all the parts of the question and pay attention to 'and' in a question, which might require you to comment on more than one aspect.
- Your opinion must be consistent and must be supported throughout your answer.
- You must write more than 250 words.
- Leave Space between each Paragraph. (Leave a line)
- Do not use single-sentence paragraphs
- Use a new paragraph for each topic

B. Different Paragraphs

Type of Question	Number of Paragraphs	Description of Paragraphs
To what extent do you agree or disagree with this statement?	4/5	1. Introduction 2. Reason why I agree/disagree 3. Another reason why I agree/disagree 4. Concession paragraph reason why I don't agree/disagree 5. Conclusion
Discuss both views and give your own opinion.	5	1. Introduction 2. One view 3. Other view 4. Your opinion 5. Conclusion
Why is this so? Give reasons for this and solutions?	5	1. Introduction 2. Reason why it is so 3. Reasons for this 4. Solutions for this 5. Conclusion
Do the disadvantages of international tourism outweigh the advantages?	4	1. Introduction (more advantages) 2. Advantages 3. Disadvantages 4. Conclusion
Why is this so? What effect does it have on the individual and the society?	5	1. Introduction 2. Why this is so 3. Effect/s on individual 4. Effect/s on society 5. Conclusion

2. FLOW OF AN ESSAY

A. Writing Introduction of an Essay

The introduction must contain a brief overview of our idea and opinion that we will take in the essay and write in the following paragraphs. The introduction of the para is a significant part. A well-written introduction can set the tone for the success of the rest of the essay.

Formula For a Perfect Introduction is Mixture of Two Things:

- First part is the paraphrasing of the question i.e., we can rephrase the question in our language and write it as introduction. **OR** try to take out the main key words from the statement of the essay and try defining those key words in the first line.

- Second part is to introduce our idea/opinion/reason etc in the introduction in mixture with the first part. **OR** you may present a plan for the essay in the second sentence.

We must blend both parts and write an original introduction without making the examiner feel that we are simply reproducing the essay question in the introduction.

B. TIPS to maintain Coherence and Cohesion in an essay

'Coherence' is the most significant aspect after format. Most students commit the gravest mistake of not writing the answer according to what the exam question requires.
They get confused and do not write according to the demands of the question. It is one of the biggest reasons for students failing to perform extraordinarily.
The meaning of coherence is 'logical and consistent' and 'forming a unified whole. In the context of writing an essay, coherence means that we need to be logical and consistent in our answers. All the paragraphs from Introduction to the conclusion must form a unified-whole answer.
Therefore, you must begin by reading the question carefully and logically analysing the question. You must read the question multiple times until you understand all the parts of the question which need a response.
After reading the question, you must know all the parts of the question you have to answer, the main opinion, idea, problem, or solution that you will explain, and an appropriate example from your personal experience if you want to include it in your answer.
Afterwards, you should quickly write some points or ideas that you will write in your essay. Once you have some pointers, you will concentrate more on writing than thinking or searching for ideas. Moreover, this technique will help you to maintain coherence.
Additionally, read the question every time before writing a new paragraph. It will ensure that you do not deviate from the topic and answer all parts.

C. Use of Connectors

Connecting words or phrases or transition words adds a flow to your answer and makes your essay cohesive. It helps you to connect your words with your idea and produce a consistent answer throughout the essay.

For Example, However, Consequently, Whereas, Nevertheless, On the other hand, Contrastingly, Despite, therefore, etc.

D. Using surveys and research to support opinion

You must use real examples and evidence from your own life experience to support your opinion. Examiners cannot check if your research and survey examples are real. Do not use memorised examples for all essays. Therefore, you must present a clear position supported by examples from your own life experience and not mention fake data or statistics.

3. GRAMMAR

Since IELTS is an English testing system, grammar is one of the essential elements to achieving high band scores. To write an attractive essay, you must write correct grammar and try not to make serious grammatical errors. Few mistakes in the response will not lead to a poor result. However, it may lead to a deduction of ½ Band. You must ensure that no grammatical errors are committed by reviewing your essay for any mistakes.

You must use punctuation carefully. It is one of the fundamental mistakes that students commit and does not use commas (,), full stops (.) or apostrophes (') correctly.

4. VOCABULARY AND SPELLINGS

Only use formal vocabulary/words in your essay. Do not use colloquial or informal expressions. Use uncommon words to show your lexical resource (vocabulary range). Use words for which you do not need to take a dictionary and find its meaning or waste valuable time thinking about their spelling in the examination.

Use your style: words in your essay must compliment your overall writing style. The biggest mistakes people commit are using stock lines to impress the examiner or memorising some lines to use in every situation to reach the word limit. Don't commit the mistake of reproducing remembered essay. You must create stock lines and examples which compliments your writing style and are relevant to the essay question.
You must make ensure that you are writing correct spellings in the examination. You must write words which you use in your day-to-day writing. Resultantly, you will commit fewer mistakes. While practising for the exam, you must identify the common spelling mistakes you commit. You should note those common mistakes and try to memorise the correct spellings. On the examination day, you must read these words to refresh your memory regarding your general spelling mistakes.

You must avoid repetition of words by using a wide range of vocabulary words instead of common words used in writing tasks. Using a range of uncommon words will help you to score a Band score higher than seven and will help you to improve your written communication.

- Use only formal words

- Use common words

- Use words relevant to topic

- Use words that you understand

- Avoid typo (typographical errors)

- Avoid spelling mistakes

- Do not use slang (awesome / funky)

- Do not use contractions (can't, doesn't, don't)

- Do not overuse synonyms (two or three synonyms are sufficient)

- Use simple words

- Use your own style

- Don't produce memorised sentences or lines

- Avoid repetition
- Do not mix up American and British spelling (You should use one or the other system)
- Do not Use a word if you don't understand it or cannot spell it.

Do not use memorised phrases such as:

- Controversial topic/hot topic
- Two-edged sword/double-edged sword/2 sides/faces of a coin
- In a nutshell
- I pen down by saying
- There are pros and cons
- This essay will discuss
- Reasons why I hold this view
- This is a highly controversial/is a highly debated issue
- Avoid proverbs and clichés – 'old is gold'

The following table contains some of the most common words or cliché words. It also provides you with words to be used in place of common words in writing an essay.

Do not use (Common words)	Use	Do not use (Common words)	Use
Nowadays	In recent times	Crux of the discussion	The main/key issue is…
Can't	Cannot	Stuff/thing	Use the correct word!
Controversial issue	Major issue	e.g.	For example, …
The pros and cons	Benefits and drawbacks	Every coin has two sides/faces	There are both disadvantages and advantages…
Firstly	The primary reason why	A double-edged sword	The solution can also cause issues as…
Secondly	Lack of education is another reason why…	In a nutshell	In conclusion…

Avoid overused phrases, idioms, proverbs, and clichés. These include phrases like:

- The grass is always greener on the other side
- Love is blind
- Off the top of my head
- Old is gold
- A friend in need is a friend indeed

5. RANGE OF SENTENCES

One of the lesser-known factors to scoring high on the IELTS writing module is the range of sentences. Usually, people ignore this factor and blame it on the IELTS testing bodies for not giving expected band scores even after using a range of vocabulary.

You should use a wide range of structures accurately to present your ideas and opinion. The Essay must have a mix of complex and simple sentences. However, your complex sentences should not be long and complicated.

6. REVIEW

Once you have completed your essay, you must review your answer for any mistakes. Moreover, you must ensure that you have achieved all the tasks in the following checklist: -

Task response	<ul><li>Did you answer ALL parts of the question properly?</li><li>Are all your ideas and support directly relevant to the question?</li><li>Did you avoid over-generalising the topic?</li><li>Does the examiner know exactly what you think, and do you present this position clearly for the whole essay?</li><li>Did you support your ideas with clear examples [not vague research and survey results]?</li><li>Did you write over 250 words?</li></ul>
Coherence and cohesion	<ul><li>Can the examiner follow your ideas easily, from the beginning of your essay to the end?</li><li>Does it progress clearly [introduction, main ideas with supporting examples, conclusion]?</li><li>Did you use a range linking words and phrases?</li></ul>

	• Did you avoid repetition and starting every sentence with a linking device [Firstly...Secondly...Thirdly]? • Did you use referencing [These issues...] and substitution [problems/issues] correctly? • Did you use sufficient paragraphs? • Did you use one paragraph to develop each idea? • Is there a clear introductory and concluding paragraph?
Lexical resource	• Did you use a range of vocabulary that is on-topic? • Did you use precise vocabulary choices? • Did you avoid memorised language, clichés [double-edged sword] and proverbs? • Did you use collocation correctly [environmental problem | global issue]? • Did you use appropriate uncommon words [detrimental to | cultural diversity | measures]? • Did you correct your spelling mistakes? • Did you check for typos? • Did you use the correct form of the word you needed [adverbs, nouns, adjectives, and verbs]?
Grammatical range and accuracy	• Did you use simple and complex structures accurately? • Did you use a range of structures [conditional, present perfect, relative clauses, modal verbs]? • Did you avoid long, complicated sentences? • Are your sentences error-free? • Did you punctuate correctly? • Did you use capital letters to start sentences and for proper nouns? • Did you use commas in your complex sentences, where needed? • Did you use full stops(.) to finish sentences?

Alternatives for the most common words and phrases used in IELTS Essays

Five alternatives to 'IF'

As long as...
As long as we go somewhere hot, I'll travel with you.

Suppose....
Suppose we went to Russia; would it be safe?

Unless...
Unless I get the time off work, I won't be able to go.

Providing / provided...
Providing I get the time off work, I'll go.

On (the) condition that...
On the condition that you pay me extra, I'll work over the weekend.

Five alternatives to 'AND'

As well as
Kyla loves singing as well as dancing.

Furthermore
Tina's a great singer. Furthermore, she can do magic tricks!

Too
Harry is a Messi fan. He likes Ronaldo too.

Also
Garry plays piano. He's also learning the guitar.

What is more
I've got all his music. what's more, I've seen him live three times.

Five alternatives to 'BUT'

However
Mary loves dogs. However, she hates cats.

Although
Although maya adores cats, she can't have one because she's allergic to them.

And yet
Kelly's got eleven cats, four dogs and a rabbit, and yet she wants more pets.

Nevertheless
Keeping horses can be very expensive. Nevertheless, I've got three of them.

Even so
My cat's old, smelly and he pees in the house. Even so, I love him to bits.

Five alternatives to 'BECAUSE'

As
I can't work this weekend as I have to look after the children.

Due to the fact that

Due to fact that this is now a play area, you may no longer park here.

Since
Since you asked nicely, I'll let you use my phone.

Owing to
Owing to bad weather, the match is off.

Now that
I can date anyone I want now that I'm single.

Five alternatives to 'ANGRY'

Cross
Please don't get cross with me. I didn't mean to hurt your feelings.

Fuming
Of course, I'm fuming, I flew first class, and the airline lost my luggage!

Enraged
My neighbor is enraged at our noisy parties. We'd better stop them for a while!

Furious
I broke my sister's computer. she's furious!

See red
If I don't finish this report soon, my boss will see red!

Five alternatives to 'THEN'

Following that
After the performances, the judges will meet. Following that, they will announce the winner.

Next
Mix the flour and eggs, next add the sugar, and finally, stir the cocoa.

After that
Turn left, then turn right. After that you'll see a roundabout. The hospital is there.

Subsequently
The product failed safety tests, subsequently, it was recalled.

Thereupon
The shooter surrendered. The police thereupon arrested him.

Five alternatives to 'GREAT'

Marvelous
I love your shoes; where did you get them? They are tremendous.

Superb
I watched a superb documentary about space travel late night.

Stunning
Have you seen Mary's artworks? It's stunning.

Stupendous
That was a stupendous meal; the best I have ever tasted.

Tremendous
That's a tremendous song. Play it again.

Five alternatives to 'IMMEDIATELY'

Without delay
Granny needs her tablets. Give them to her without delay.

Straight away
When I noticed the door was not locked, I knew straight away we'd been burgled.

Instantly
The pilot was killed instantly when the helicopter crashed.

Pronto
It's late; get the report finished pronto!

At once
'Come here at once, Jos!' said the mother.

Five alternatives to 'INTERESTING'

Fascinating
The dinosaur exhibition is completely fascinating.

Intriguing
I find police documentation most intriguing.

Engaging
The way she gazes into the camera is very engaging.

Captivating
Kori's poems are captivating; I need all of them repeatedly.

Compelling
The actor gave a compelling performance and received positive reviews.

Five alternatives to 'VERY BIG'

Vast
Russia is a vast country.

Gigantic
I want a gigantic cake for my birthday, so all my friends can have a piece.

Humungous
Don't go in the bathroom. There's a humungous spider in there!

Huge
I've just caught a huge fish!

Massive
She's just bought a massive truck. I don't know how she is going to park it anywhere!

Five alternatives to 'TIRED'

Spent
I've been working hard this week. I'm spent.

Exhausted
When the marathon ended, the young athlete was exhausted.

Knackered
Betty partied all night. In the morning, she was knackered.

Worn out
I can't babysit any more. Children are a handful and I'm worn out!

On my last legs
No more bargain hunting today. I'm on my last legs. Let's go home.

Four alternatives to 'THANK YOU'.

you really shouldn't have!
That's such a nice present; you really shouldn't have!

You're too kind
You're playing for lunch? Oh, you're too kind!

Cheers
Cheers for that; it's helpful!

Much appreciated
Your work here is much appreciated.

Five alternatives to 'APPROXIMATELY'

About
That job's quite easy. It should only take about half an hour.

Around
The traffic was bad. It took around an hour to get here.

More or less
To make this recipe you will need a liter of milk, more or less.

In the region of
That new restaurant is so expensive! We spent in the region of $400 there last night!

Let's say
He was, let's say, two meters tall!

Four alternatives to 'CHILD'

Little ones
The adults are having wine and there's apple juice for the little ones.

Youngster
I loved riding my bike when I was a youngster.

Kid
Mary's just a kid; she's not allowed to work.

Young'un
Can I have a child seat for the young'un?

Five alternatives to 'WHY'

How come
How come I don't get a turn?

How is it that
How is it that he got the job, and I didn't?

Tell me the reason
Can someone tell me the reason we use the present perfect here?

What's the point of
What's the point of talking to you? You never listen!

What for
Call you? What for? You never answer!

Five alternatives to 'YES'

Go on then
Go on then; I'll babysit for you this evening.

If you insist
Another glass of wine? If you insist.

Absolutely
Am I a Ronaldo fan? Absolutely!

Works for me
You want to finish the report while I update the spreadsheet? Works for me.

I'm in
free drinks after work? I'm in.

Five alternatives to 'SO'

That means
It's sunny! That means we can go to the beach.

And now
I got up early, and now I'm really tired.
Because of that
There was an accident and because of that, I was late.

Which made
He shouted at me, which made me angry.

As a result
It rained all day and as a result, water came through the roof.

Five alternatives to 'OLD'

Ancient
There is an ancient monument just off the main road.

Aged
My aged parents will be staying with me over the summer.

Antiquated
I'm not sure this antiquated equipment will work well enough for this job.

Getting on a bit
My dog's getting on a bit, but he still loves his morning walks!

Mature
This dress style suits the mature lady.

Five alternatives to 'VERY'

Incredibly
Formula one cars are incredibly fast.

Terribly
I find history exams terribly difficult. I always do terribly bad in them.

Horrifically
That news was horrifically sad.

Fantastically
She played fantastically well in the match. She was the reason that they won!

Hugely
The results of this study are hugely significant.

Five alternatives to 'VERY SAD'

Gutted
I was gutted that I couldn't come to your wedding.

Devastated
I've got to get a new goldfish today; the kids would be devastated if they knew the old one had died!

Desolate
Mary is desolate following her divorce.

Inconsolable
Lee failed all his exams; he's inconsolable!

A broken (wo)man
Harry lost his job after 20 years and now he's a broken man.

Top-Notch words for IELTS Writing

1. In order to

Usage: "In order to" can be used to introduce an explanation for the purpose of an argument.
Example: "In order to understand Physics, we need first to understand Maths."

2. In other words
Usage: Use "in other words" when you want to express something in a different way (more simply), to make it easier to understand, or to emphasise or expand on a point.
Example: "Frogs are amphibians. In other words, they live on the land and in the water."

3. To put it another way
Usage: This phrase is another way of saying "in other words", and can be used in particularly complex points, when you feel that an alternative way of wording a problem may help the reader achieve a better understanding of its significance.
Example: "Plants rely on photosynthesis. To put it another way, they will die without the sun."

4. That is to say
Usage: "That is" and "that is to say" can be used to add further detail to your explanation, or to be more precise.
Example: "Whales are mammals. That is to say, they must breathe air."

5. To that end
Usage: Use "to that end" or "to this end" in a similar way to "in order to" or "so".
Example: "Zoologists have long sought to understand how animals communicate with each other. To that end, a new study has been launched that looks at elephant sounds and their possible meanings."

Adding additional information to support a point
Candidates often make the mistake of using synonyms of "and" each time they want to add further information in support of a point they're making, or to build an argument. Here are some cleverer ways of doing this.

6. Moreover
Usage: Employ "moreover" at the start of a sentence to add extra information in support of a point you're making.
Example: "Moreover, the results of a recent piece of research provide compelling evidence in support of..."

7. Furthermore
Usage: This is also generally used at the start of a sentence, to add extra information.
Example: "Furthermore, there is evidence to suggest that..."

8. What's more
Usage: This is used in the same way as "moreover" and "furthermore".
Example: "What's more, this isn't the only evidence that supports this hypothesis."

9. Likewise
Usage: Use "likewise" when you want to talk about something that agrees with what you've just mentioned.
Example: "Scholar A believes X. Likewise; Scholar B argues compellingly in favour of this point of view."

10. Similarly
Usage: Use "similarly" in the same way as "likewise".
Example: "Audiences at the time reacted with shock to Beethoven's new work because it was very different to what they were used to. Similarly, we tend to react with surprise to the unfamiliar."

11. Another key thing to remember
Usage: Use the phrase "another key point to remember" or "another key fact to remember" to introduce additional facts without using the word "also".

Example: "As a Romantic, Brian was a proponent of a closer relationship between humans and nature. Another key point to remember is that Brian was writing during the Industrial Revolution, which had a major impact on the world around him."

12. As well as
Usage: Use "as well as" instead of "also" or "and".
Example: "Scholar A argued that this was due to X, as well as Y."

13. Not only… but also
Usage: This wording is used to add an extra piece of information, often something that's in some way more surprising or unexpected than the first piece of information.
Example: "Not only did Edmund Hillary have the honour of being the first to reach the summit of Everest, but he was also appointed Knight Commander of the Order of the British Empire."

14. Coupled with
Usage: Used when considering two or more arguments at a time.
Example: "Coupled with the literary evidence, the statistics paint a compelling view of…"

15. Firstly, secondly, thirdly…
Usage: This can be used to structure an argument, presenting facts clearly one after the other.
Example: "There are many points in support of this view. Firstly, X. Secondly, Y. And thirdly, Z.

16. Not to mention/to say nothing of
Usage: "Not to mention" and "to say nothing of" can be used to add extra information with a bit of emphasis.
Example: "The war caused unprecedented suffering to millions of people, not to mention its impact on the country's economy."

Words and phrases for demonstrating contrast
When you're developing an argument, you will often need to present contrasting or opposing opinions or evidence – "it could show this, but it could also show this", or "X says this, but Y disagrees". This section covers words you can use instead of the "but".

17. However
Usage: Use "however" to introduce a point that disagrees with what you've just said.
Example: "Scholar A thinks this. However, Scholar B reached a different conclusion."

18. On the other hand
Usage: Usage of this phrase includes introducing a contrasting interpretation of the same piece of evidence, a different piece of evidence that suggests something else, or an opposing opinion.
Example: "The historical evidence appears to suggest a clear-cut situation. On the other hand, the archaeological evidence presents a somewhat less straightforward picture of what happened that day."

19. Having said that
Usage: Used in a similar manner to "on the other hand" or "but".
Example: "I love going to mountains for leisure. Having said I also enjoy the city life."

20. By contrast / in comparison
Usage: Use "by contrast" or "in comparison" when you're comparing and contrasting pieces of evidence.
Example: "Scholar A's opinion, then, is based on insufficient evidence. By contrast, Scholar B's opinion seems more reasonable."

21. Then again
Usage: Use this to cast doubt on an assertion.
Example: "Writer A asserts that this was the reason for what happened. Then again, it's possible that he was being paid to say this."

22. That said
Usage: This is used in the same way as "then again".

Example: "The evidence ostensibly appears to point to this conclusion. That said, much of the evidence is unreliable at best."

23. Yet
Usage: Use this when you want to introduce a contrasting idea.
Example: "Much of scholarship has focused on this evidence. Yet not everyone agrees that this is the most important aspect of the situation."

Adding a proviso or acknowledging reservations

Sometimes, you may need to acknowledge a short falling in a piece of evidence or add a condition. Here are some ways of doing so.

24. Despite this
Usage: Use "despite this" or "in spite of this" when you want to outline a point that stands regardless of a short falling in the evidence.
Example: "The sample size was small, but the results were important despite this."

25. With this in mind
Usage: Use this when you want your reader to consider a point in the knowledge of something else.
Example: "We've seen that the methods used in the 19th century study did not always live up to the demanding standards expected in scientific research today, which makes it difficult to draw definite conclusions. With this in mind, let's look at a more recent study to see how the results compare."

26. Provided that
Usage: This means "on condition that". You can also say "providing that" or just "providing" to mean the same thing.
Example: "We may use this as evidence to support our argument, provided that we bear in mind the limitations of the methods used to obtain it."

27. In view of / in light of
Usage: These phrases are used when something has shed light on something else.
Example: "In light of the evidence from the 2013 study, we have a better understanding of…"

28. Nonetheless
Usage: This is like "despite this".
Example: "The study had its limitations, but it was nonetheless ground-breaking for its day."

29. Nevertheless
Usage: This is the same as "nonetheless".
Example: "The study was flawed, but it was important nevertheless."

30. Notwithstanding
Usage: This is another way of saying "nonetheless".
Example: "Notwithstanding the limitations of the methodology used, it was an important study in the development of how we view the workings of the human mind."

Giving examples
Here are a couple of other ways of saying for example.

31. For instance
Example: "Some birds migrate to avoid harsher winter climates. Swallows, for instance, leave the UK in early winter and fly south…"

32. To give an illustration
Example: "To give an illustration of what I mean, let's look at the case of…"

Signifying importance

When you want to demonstrate that a point is particularly important, there are several ways of highlighting it as such.

33. Significantly
Usage: Used to introduce a point that is loaded with meaning that might not be immediately apparent.
Example: "Significantly, the government is now planning to curtail crime in the city."

34. Notably
Usage: This can be used to mean "significantly" (as above), and it can also be used interchangeably with "in particular" (the example below demonstrates the first of these ways of using it).
Example: "Actual figures are notably absent from Scholar A's analysis."

35. Importantly
Usage: Use "importantly" interchangeably with "significantly".
Example: "Importantly, Scholar A was being employed by X when he wrote this work and was presumably therefore under pressure to portray the situation more favourably than he perhaps might otherwise have done."

Summarising

Here are some words and phrases to help you summarize your essay.

36. In conclusion
Usage: Typically used to introduce the concluding paragraph or sentence of an essay, summarising what you've discussed in a broad overview.
Example: "In conclusion, the evidence points almost exclusively to Argument A."

37. Above all
Usage: Used to signify what you believe to be the most significant point, and the main takeaway from the essay.
Example: "Above all, it seems pertinent to remember that…"

38. Persuasive
Usage: This is a useful word to use when summarising which argument, you find most convincing.
Example: "Scholar A's point – that Constanza Mozart was motivated by financial gain – seems to me to be the most persuasive argument for her actions following Mozart's death."

39. Compelling
Usage: Use in the same way as "persuasive" above.
Example: "The most compelling argument is presented by Scholar A."

40. All things considered
Usage: This means "taking everything into account".
Example: "All things considered; it seems reasonable to assume that…"

Useful Vocab and Templates for the Essays

Useful vocabulary / phrases to open / start the essay:

- Many/some people claim/opine/believe that...

- There is no denying that...

- It is often said that...

- These days.../ Nowadays.../ In this day and age...

- It goes without saying that...

- It is universally accepted that...

- We live in an age when many of us are...

- People are divided in their opinion regarding...

- .... is one of the most important issues...

- Whether .... or .... is a controversial issue...

Useful vocabulary/phrases to end the Introduction part:

- Let us examine both views before reaching a concrete decision.

- The following paragraphs discuss whether ...... or ...... and reach a reasonable conclusion.

- The following essay takes a look at both sides of the argument.

- My two cents go for...

- However, I strongly believe that...

- I oppose the view and my reasons will be explained in the following paragraphs.

- I will support this view with arguments in the following paragraphs.

- I personally believe that...

- Thus, the advantages far outweigh the disadvantages...

- I wholeheartedly believe that this trend should be changed.

Vocabulary for the opinion part:

- In my opinion...

- I strongly opine that...

- I strongly agree with the idea that...

- I strongly disagree with the given topic...

- I think...

- My opinion is that...

- Personally speaking...

- In my view...

- I believe...

- Apparently...

- Personally speaking...

- According to me...

- From my point of view... (Not 'In my point of view')

- As far as I am concerned...

- From my perspective...

- I realise...

- To my way of thinking...

- It seems to me that...

- To me...

- To my mind...

- My own view on the matter is...

- It appears that...

- I feel that...

- I understand...

- I suppose...

Vocabulary for the 2nd paragraph Part:

- It is true that...

- First...

- First of all...

- Firstly...

- First and foremost...

- Initially...

- To begin with...

- To start with...

- Let us take a look at...

- It is worth considering...

- In the first place...

- Though it is true that...

- Some people believe that...

- Many people think that...

- According to many...

- Some people believe that...

- Many supports the view that...

- On the one hand...

Vocabulary for the 3rd, 4th ...... paragraph Part:

- Second(ly)... (Not 'Second of all')

- Third(ly)...

- Then...

- Next...

- After that...

- And...

- Again...

- Also...

- Besides...

- Likewise...

- In addition...

- Consequently...

- What's more...

- Furthermore...

- Moreover...

- Other people think that...

- Other people believe that...

- On the other hand...

- Apart from that...

- Finally...

- Last but not least...

Vocabulary to show the comparison:

- In the same way...

- Likewise...

- Similarly...

- Like the previous point...

- Similar to...

- Also...

- At the same time...

- Just as...

Vocabulary to show contrast:

- On the other hand...

- On the contrary...

- However...

- Nevertheless.../ Nonetheless...

- But...

- Oppositely...

- Alternatively...

- Unlike...

- While...

- Whilst...

- Although...

- Though...

- Even though...

- Despite... / In spite of...

- In spite of the fact that...

- Alternatively...

- In contrast to this...

- Then again...

- On the other hand...

81

- Despite the fact that...

- Even so...

- Yet...

- With respect to...

- In terms of...

Vocabulary to show an example:

- As an example...

- For instance...

- For example...

- Like...

- As...

- Among others...

- Such as...

- Particularly...

- Regarding...

- In particular...

- Namely...

- With respect to...

- As far .... is concerned...

- To show an example...

- To give an example...

- To cite an example...

- As a piece of evidence...

- To illustrate...

- To paraphrase...

- An example is...

- ...could be a good/ideal example here

- A case...

- When it comes to...

Phrases to introduce more ideas/ examples:

- Furthermore...

- In addition...

- On top of that...

- Besides...

- What is more...

- Another point worth noting is...

- Another factor to consider is...

- Furthermore...

- Not only .... but also...

- Also...

Vocabulary to show consequence, effects or result:

- As a result...

- Consequently...

- As a consequent...

- As an effect...

- Thus...

- So...

- The reason why...

- Therefore...

- On account of...

- Because of...

- Hence...

- Eventually...

- For this/that reason...

- Thereby...

- Due to...

- Owing to...

Vocabulary to present an idea:

- Research shows that...

- Research has found that...

- When it comes to...

Vocabulary to show result & reason:

- As a result...
- As a result of...
- Due to...
- One reason behind this is...
- ... has led to/ ... has resulted in...
- Consequently...
- Therefore...

Vocabulary to sum up at the end of a paragraph:

- To sum up...
- In short...
- In a word...
- To put it simply...
- That is to say...
- To repeat in short...
- To summarise...

Vocabulary to make a point stronger/ Adding emphasis:

- It goes without saying that...
- Obviously...
- Needless to say...
- There is little doubt that...
- Must... After
- After all...
- Even if...
- Therefore...
- Thus.....

Vocabulary for clarifying or rephrasing:

- To put it simply...

- To put in another way...
- That is to say...
- In other words...

Other transitional words/connective words:

- Then...
- Else...
- Otherwise...
- Besides...
- As soon as...
- As much as.....

Vocabulary for the conclusion part:

- In conclusion...
- In summary...
- To conclude...
- To conclude with...
- To sum up...
- In general...
- To summarise...
- In short...
- All in all...
- Overall...
- To draw the conclusion...
- To elucidate ('To elucidate' means - 'make something clear' or 'to explain'.)
- All things considered...
- By and large...
- Taking everything into consideration...
- Taking everything into account...

Weighing up both sides of the argument.

TASK 1

These days huge portions of population are moving from rural areas to urban areas. Do you think it is a positive or a negative trend?

The majority of the world's population resides in rural areas. The working population between the ages of 18 to 40 are rising in the rural areas. Therefore, young individuals are moving towards cities in search of education and jobs.

The population pressure on the countryside has resulted in fewer work opportunities. Moreover, in villages, people depend on agriculture for their earnings due to very few other jobs. Governments around the globe are bringing rules and regulations to distribute the human population equally between rural and urban areas, which has resulted in people moving to urban areas. On the other hand, cities are in shortage of labour and need workers for several needs. Thus, to meet the demand for human capital, the governments are taking steps to encourage people to migrate by creating new job opportunities in cities. In my city, Toronto, the movement of the new population has brought various positive changes. The household income of nearby rural areas and literacy rates have soared. Additionally, the living standards of the people in the countryside of Toronto have improved with the increase in income.

Furthermore, cities have advanced infrastructure to support education and health. Less opportunity for higher education, poor transportation, and no self-employment opportunities in rural areas are more factors for people moving to urban areas. These reasons have encouraged people to relocate to improve their lives.

In my opinion, migration to cities has become necessary for all the communities as cities are more developed. Therefore, moving people to cities has more advantages than disadvantages.

255 Words

Vocab for Task 1:

1. Countryside- rural area
2. Literacy – educated
3. Soared – rise
4. Relocate – change

TASK 2

Tourism is becoming increasingly important as a source of revenue to many countries, but its disadvantages should not be overlooked. To what extent do you agree or disagree?

Across the globe, tourism is quickly becoming one of the leading income sources in the overall earnings of a country. The advancement achieved in means of transportation is resulting in a high number of travellers, which creates many problems for the country and its local population.

The problems with the travel industry are complex and have given rise to cultural conflicts in various places. Since tourists are not aware of the customs and traditions of the local people, it often results in confrontations between tourists and locals. Locals regularly blame tourists for not respecting historical and religious sites. This often leads to disappointing experiences for some visitors and the locals. The worsening situation of law and order is difficult to manage at leading attractions owing to frequent scams by locals.

Furthermore, development of the holiday business is a leading reason for higher emission levels of pollution at tourist places. On my recent visit to Italy, I experienced this from the presence of dirty and stinking water streams in Venice and its dying marine life due to many cruise ships standing at its ports.

On the other hand, numerous South-Asian nations are benefiting from the soaring number of tourists in their region. Tourism has improved the living standards of the locals and uplifted numerous communities out of poverty in Asian countries.

It is undeniable that the travelling industry is impacting positively as well as negatively on many people's social and economic circles. However, administrations must follow a cautious approach to keep a check on over-tourism to ensure that tourism grows to benefit all the people.

264 Words

Vocab for Task-2

1. Conflicts – clashes
2. Confrontations – encounter
3. Stinking – foul odour
4. Undeniable – evident
5. Cautious – careful

TASK 3

Some people think that foreign visitors should be charged more than locals when they visit cultural and tourist attractions in a country. To what extent do you agree with this view?

AGREE:

Across the globe, charging higher prices from tourists at attractions and public places is a common practice. This system generates more funds for the development of cultural sites, but it also promotes a sense of bias towards foreigners.

Governments try to justify the higher costs for visitors by stating that outsiders do not pay local taxes and that locals are contributing to the country by paying various taxes. Thus, travellers are charged heavily for using facilities at tourist locations provided by the government. This practice is also logical as holidaymakers may only travel once or twice to these places in their lifetime and do not have any issue paying more. Besides, travellers have more resources at their disposal to spend during their holidays than locals. Charging fewer amounts from residents allows them to connect with their ancient traditions and promotes a sense of pride in their country.

Additionally, imposing more sums of money on travellers make sure that the attractions are maintained and can handle a high number of visitors. It also helps in developing the basic facilities to provide a comfortable and memorable experience to visitors. This also helps to subsidise the ticket prices for the locals. Nevertheless, charging too much may prevent outsiders from visiting such places. Resultantly, it can lead to lower income for the economy.

Tourist attractions are an opportunity to showcase the history, culture, and traditions of a society. Therefore, charging higher fees to foreigners must be balanced in order to promote tourist attractions. Moreover, it must not prevent the majority of foreigners from visiting the landmarks.

262 Words

Vocab for Task – 3

1. Bias – favouritism
2. Imposing – commanding

TASK 4

Some people think that foreign visitors should be charged more than locals when they visit cultural and tourist attractions in a country. To what extent do you agree with this view?

DISAGREE :

Generally, countries levy more entry fees on foreign tourists when they visit places of interest in comparison to local vacationers. However, such a system is unfair since it burdens overseas visitors with higher expenses as well as discourages them from visiting these locations.

Since the attractions are a great opportunity for a nation to showcase its historical wealth to international travellers, they must be greeted at such cultural sites with open arms. Exorbitant entry fees may act as a deterrent for foreigners from touring such places. Therefore, lower turnouts will lead to reduced proceeds for the economy. Further, differential charges for exploring the same place can endorse a feeling of discontent and discrimination among holidaymakers. Thus, if all the sightseers are equally charged, it will lead to spreading the message of equality and promote the welfare image of the nation at international forums. Thereby bringing in more revenue to the reserves of the exchequer.

Additionally, if charges are kept similar for everyone, travellers will be able to explore more locations at economical costs. Hence, they will have extra resources to spend on indigenous businesses.

Nevertheless, administrations may tend to justify charging extravagant amounts for admission to various tourist sites on outsiders. They term it as fair towards locals who are already paying taxes to the government for the expenditure required for the development of cultural sites.

The state must follow all safeguards to ensure that tourists are not charged higher than locals as it may precipitate feelings of alienation. Moreover, equality will ensure economic growth and promote local cultural values.

260 Words

Vocab for Task – 4

1. Vacationers – travellers
2. Exorbitant - excessive
3. Deterrent – warning
4. Turnouts – crowds
5. Endorse – approve
6. Discontent – unhappiness
7. Forums – mediums
8. Exchequer – treasury / government's fund
9. Indigenous – native
10. Tend – incline
11. Extravagant – excessive
12. Safeguards – precautions
13. Alienation – disaffection

TASK 5

Children nowadays spend a great deal of time on e-learning. However, television or computers cannot replace the book as a learning tool, which is why children are less well educated today. To what extent do you agree with this statement?

I believe in an old saying that 'books are a man's best friend'. However, with technological advancement, this saying is fast becoming a thing of the past as the majority of people are shifting to audio-visual means for learning and entertainment.

Due to recent pandemics around the globe, social distancing rules have forced our education system to switch online to teach kids. Thus, children are spending more time on screens rather than reading books. Moreover, the quality of education is suffering, and children are learning fewer things. Students opting for electronic means for gaining knowledge are failing to develop a culture of reading books and are lagging behind their friends, who adhere to traditional methods. People in the olden times had fewer means to keep their children occupied. Hence, the best way to entertain and teach new things was to introduce them to books.

Additionally, continuous sitting in front of screens for long hours can be physically as well as mentally tiring. Parents must encourage their children to read books to improve their concentration levels and academic grades.

Besides, from my ten years of teaching experience, I can conclude that the rate of students failing in their secondary classes has risen considerably since the introduction of e-learning methods. I reckon that electronic screens might not yet replace books as a learning tool, as these mediums have only limited applications to teach new things.

E-learning techniques have a limited scope of imparting knowledge as it is in the developing stage, which cannot satisfy the desires of youngsters to learn different subjects. Nevertheless, we must endeavour to use both sources of knowledge while considering our children's educational needs.

276 Words

Vocab for Task - 5

1. Pandemics – outbreak
2. Switch – alter
3. Opting – decide
4. Olden – ancient
5. Adhere – follow
6. Scope – possibility
7. Imparting – offering
8. Endeavour – efforts

TASK 6

Every one of us should become vegetarian because eating meat can cause serious health problems. To what extent do you agree or disagree?

It is a long-debated issue whether a person should include meat in his or her daily nutrition or live on a plant-based diet. Moreover, the bigger dilemma is, which regime has more health benefits?

The decision to remove meat from our daily diet may not prove to be the healthiest option for everyone. People indulged in rigorous mental or physical activities can never survive on a plain vegan diet. A vegetarian diet cannot provide the required nourishment for the proper functioning of the human body since it lacks the variety of nutrients found in meat. Consequently, one must include animal protein for a healthy diet. I remember during a science lesson in high school, we were informed that meat consumption assists in building muscles and generates new white blood cells, which boosts immunity levels. Therefore, I never thought of excluding meat from my diet in order to keep my fitness levels high.

In our present world, people are devoting their efforts to adopting healthy eating habits to lead a better life which is the leading cause for people rapidly moving to veganism. A vegan diet generally has fewer harmful effects on the digestive system as vegan food items are digested easily than meat products. A plant-only diet contains no fat, which helps a person to live longer.

We cannot ignore all the health advantages of meat consumption in light of a few health issues since the vegan diet cannot provide all the required nutrients for sustainable living. Therefore, I reckon it is not practical to become vegetarian for everyone.

259 Words

Vocab for Task - 6

1. Dilemma – difficulty
2. Regime – routine
3. Indulge – involve
4. Rigorous – harsh
5. Nourishment – nutrition
6. Consequently – therefore
7. Devoting - allotting
8. Rapidly – swiftly
9. In light of – considering
10. Sustainable – viable
11. Reckon – look upon

TASK 7

Some people believe money is the best gift for the teenagers while others disagree. Discuss both views and give your own opinion.

Selecting a present is always one of the challenging tasks, and it is even more problematic and confusing when the gift is for a teenager. Therefore, can giving money be the ultimate solution to this problem? Let us try to find the answer.

Most people consider handing out cash as the best possible gift for adolescents. After all, no one is ever dissatisfied while receiving money. In many cultures, giving out cash to kids is an acceptable practice. At various celebrations, when children step into adulthood, guests are expected to give out money as gifts. Since the preferences of teenagers may change rapidly, it becomes impossible to give an appropriate item as per their liking. Additionally, dishing out cash to the teenagers is a significant opportunity to teach critical life skills in financial planning.

Nevertheless, the idea of money as a gift may be seen as a shallow tradition in some societies as many people tend to give a personalised gift to convey their emotions to their loved ones. Moreover, an unrestrained amount of money in the hands of teenagers can become a grave issue as children may fall into bad habits of excessive buying.

Giving money as a present is always the best option as it provides freedom to the recipient to utilise the cash-on-hand according to their wishes. I remember during my childhood days, whenever a relative gave me money on my birthdays, I used to be happy more than any other gift.

I reckon we must teach our young generation about the values of presenting individualised gifts. However, as far as the perfect gift is concerned, money has no substitute.

273 Words

Vocab for Task – 7

1. Challenging – difficult
2. Problematic – tricky
3. Ultimate – eventual
4. Handing out – sharing
5. Adolescents – teen
6. Critical - important
7. Shallow tradition – empty
8. Personalised – customised
9. Unrestrained – uncontrollable
10. Grave – serious
11. Excessive – too much
12. Recipient – receiver
13. Substitute – alternative

TASK 8

Art forms such as music, paintings, sculptures, etc. are a way of expressing human emotions which cannot be expressed in words and gestures. It is the expression of the artist about what he feels and sees of the world. Do you think Government should spend money on promotion of Art?

Around the globe, various performers have captured human emotions ranging from love to jealousy through their different art forms. It is of great importance that the administrations must promote art as it is the exhibition of the artist's understanding and feedback of the world.

Art has the potential to attract wealthy tourists, which contributes to the betterment of the local economy through increased revenues and by creating new work opportunities for locals. On my recent vacation to Italy, I observed that the Italian government is earning enormous revenue from a high number of travellers to the city of Rome in search of ancient art and crafts. The Administration promotes art by incurring immense expenditure on advertising at the international level. Similarly, I visited the metropolis to enjoy various activities such as opera, painting, and other performing arts after being induced by an illustrious advertisement in a travel magazine.

If authorities spend their resources on the promotion of art, it will be an effective tool for glorifying the nation's culture and history at various international and domestic levels. Fine art assists a country in establishing cultural supremacy and is a way to show the power of the intellect to the world and super-nations. Since artists have always described the hardships and pleasures of ordinary people through their art, we can learn about the history and culture of humankind through it.

Therefore, the state must spend resources on improving the artists and their art, which can establish the cultural domination of a country. Moreover, it will be a source of income for its economy.

262 Words

Vocab for Task-8

1. Captured – acquired
2. Potential – promising
3. Enormous – huge
4. Incurring- suffering
5. Immense – extremely large
6. Metropolis – major city
7. Induced – tempted
8. Illustrious – memorable
9. Glorifying –adoring
10. Assists – help
11. Supremacy – dominancy
12. Intellect – ability

TASK 9

The age at which people are now having children has risen. Some people believe that because of this, the families and the countries will suffer some problems.
What is your opinion?

The average age at which parents conceive a kid is alarmingly high. It is causing numerous difficulties for parents as well as adversely affecting the balance of the country's working population.

In yesteryears, married couples were not mindful of family planning measures and the consequences of having a pregnancy at a young age. Therefore, with growing awareness about health implications and economic factors, in recent times, the average age of couples who have kids is rising across the globe. The focus on career and to attain a certain financial level for enormous expenses associated with childcare is causing the upward swing in the age at which parents have children. Additionally, in some conservative societies, mothers are subject to ridicule or stigma for having a kid early and face problems in getting high-paid jobs.

The foremost challenge with the advancement of age is that the fertility rate of humans declines with ageing. Consequently, they face various complexities while conceiving a baby naturally. Further, mothers are often subject to post-natal health complications, which in some cases may be fatal for them or their child's life. Moreover, in some situations, older parents may not be able to cope-up with the energy levels of young kids.

Countries are experiencing economic meltdowns due to delayed pregnancies. Some states are in a phase where the count of the working population is less than the number of dependents. Thus, putting an extra burden on the government exchequers to pay pensions and other welfare payments to retirees.

The proneness to have kids during the later stages of life has numerous drawbacks. Therefore, measures should be taken immediately by the authorities and communities, keeping in view the holistic development of children and the country's economic targets.

287 Words

Vocab for Task – 9

1. Conceive – perceive
2. Alarmingly – dangerously
3. Adversely – unfavourably
4. Yesteryears – the past
5. Consequences – result of
6. Attain – accomplish
7. Enormous – huge
8. Upward – higher
9. Conservative – traditional
10. Ridicule – mockery
11. Stigma – shame
12. Foremost – first in order
13. Fertility rate – pregnancy chances
14. Complexities – complications
15. Post-natal – after birth
16. Complications – difficulties
17. Exchequers – treasury / government funds
18. Proneness – tendency
19. Holistic – complete

TASK 10

The most effective way to solve traffic and transport problems in the cities is to encourage people from cities to live in suburbs or the countryside. To what extent do you agree or disagree?

Over the last century, major cities of all countries have seen exponential growth in population and unabated migration from rural areas. As a result, unprecedented transportation issues within the city limits lead to traffic snarls, accidents, and a scarcity of parking spaces.

The solution to commuter traffic to force people out of the urban areas is impractical and insufficient since it fails to address the key issues to solve traffic snarls. If people stand displaced to the countryside, more people will move to the city, and the traffic situation will remain unsolved. Therefore, we must strengthen the transportation options such as buses or trains capable of ferrying masses, which will help to reduce the number of private vehicles on roads. The existing public carriage system must be expanded to nearby towns so that the public conveniently access cities, as it will encourage them to reside outside municipal areas.

Additionally, to diminish the number of cars on roads and inspire people to share rides with others, the government must incentivise people to carpool by creating special lanes for people having more than one person in a vehicle and giving them subsidies on tolls. Private automobiles must be taxed highly to encourage people to use mass transit. However, fair distribution of residents in various areas will ensure the development of all the regions and help effectively solve transportation troubles.

Moving the people out of cities cannot resolve the menace of an inferior transportation system. Therefore, the government must take radical steps to mitigate the traffic woes.

254 Words

Vocab for Task -10

1. Exponential – growing
2. Unabated – non-stop
3. Unprecedented – exceptional
4. Snarls – mess
5. Scarcity – deficiency
6. Impractical – unrealistic
7. Insufficient - lacking
8. Displaced – disturbed
9. Ferrying – transporting
10. Carriage – carrying
11. Conveniently – easily
12. Diminish – decline
13. Incentivise – encourage
14. Subsides – assistance
15. Menace – danger / hazard
16. Inferior – secondary
17. Mitigate – lessen
18. Woes – sufferings

TASK 11

In many places, new homes are needed, but the only space available for building them is the countryside. Some people believe it is more important to protect the countryside and not build new homes there. What is your opinion about this?

Major cities across the globe are reeling under population pressure due to uncontrolled migration. Thus, the government is developing new settlements in rural areas, which may cause harmful effects on the natural habitat of the countryside.

The construction of new homes on the outskirts of the cities causes the clearing of fields and cutting down of forests. Consequently, both methods contribute to destroying the ecological balance of rural areas. Deforestation can cause numerous unnatural phenomena such as famines, irregular rains, and changes in crop cycles. The development of rural places may cause an increase in pollution levels, which may destroy the natural environment and pave the way for various health problems for its inhabitants. Measures must be focused on optimum utilisation of residential spaces to settle maximum people, which will keep the countryside undisturbed.

Since many metropolises have limited land for construction, people expand to nearby rural areas to build new residencies. Lower land prices in the country will attract many new inhabitants able to afford a house and build a life in the vicinity of a larger city. Developing new areas is an opportunity to create more jobs while reducing pressure on the infrastructure of nearby municipalities.

I reckon, to ensure no rural areas are acquired to develop new dwelling units, administrations must endeavour to create high rises within municipal areas or promote community living systems to accommodate people within the city.

Building residential units in the countryside come at environmental and economic costs. Therefore, the government should take all the necessary measures to develop sustainable living options in cities.

261 Words

Vocab for Task -11

1. Reeling – winding
2. Settlements – arrangement
3. Habitat – environment
4. Countryside – rural area
5. Outskirts – area outside the cities
6. Ecological – eco-friendly
7. Famines – scarcity
8. Optimum – best
9. Metropolises – major city
10. Vicinity – local area
11. Acquired – captured
12. Dwelling – house
13. Endeavour – attempt
14. Sustainable – viable

TASK 12

Today more and more tourists are visiting places where conditions are difficult, such as the Sahara Desert or the Antarctic. What are the benefits and disadvantages for tourists who visit such places?

Across the globe, the trend of planning holidays to exotic destinations is rising. People are visiting places which may not be considered tourist's hotspots in the traditional sense, such as high mountain peaks, cold deserts, and far-flung deserted islands.

The terms vagabond, digital nomads, and backpackers are synonymous with the new class of wanderers keen on exploring unconventional places. This movement is an opportunity for tourists to understand and empathise with the daily difficulties of people living in these areas with limited resources. It helps in understanding a variety of cultures and promotes harmony among communities. During a vacation in the 'Great Himalayas' in India, my car developed some problems while passing through a remote hamlet; I was overwhelmed by the generosity of the locals. They helped me to repair my car and offered food and accommodation. Moreover, people are also earning enormous amounts through travel videos. They encapsulate these places in their memoirs and use these are financial gains.

On the contrary, the influx of sightseers to far-flung places deteriorates the equilibrium of ecologically sensitive areas. The polluting of pristine environment often by travellers cause irreparable loss to the sites. Furthermore, tourists are often surprised by the unpredictable weather conditions, and to add to their woes, accommodation options are limited, which leads to unpleasant experiences. In case of medical emergencies, the life of the distressed tourist may be at risk due to challenges posed by the lack of facilities at difficult locations.

I reckon individuals must be at liberty to explore the greatness of nature as it has numerous rewards. However, before visiting any such terrain, we must take all the necessary training and precautions for safe travelling.

279 Words

Vocab for Task -12

1. Exotic – unusual
2. Hotspots – famous tourist places
3. Wanderer – adventurer
4. Exploring – wandering
5. Unconventional – odd
6. Empathise – sympathise / understand
7. Harmony- social agreement
8. Hamlet – suburb
9. Generosity – kindness
10. Overwhelmed – stunned
11. Encapsulate – encase
12. Memoirs – journals
13. Influx – flow
14. Sightseers – tourist
15. Deteriorates – degrade
16. Equilibrium – balance
17. Ecological – environmental
18. Sensitive – delicate
19. pristine – pure
20. unpredictable – uncertain
21. woes – sufferings
22. distressed – upset
23. liberty – freedom
24. terrain – landscape
25. precautions – carefulness

TASK 13

Some people say that parents should encourage their children to take part in organised group activities in their free time. Others say that it is important for children to learn how to occupy themselves on their own. Discuss both these views and give your own opinion.

Parents attempt to organise their kids' activities to utilise their leisure time productively. Generally, folks encourage their wards to indulge in team events to improve their interpersonal skills. However, some people persuade their kids to uptake individual activities to teach competencies to rely on themselves in every situation.

Since organised group activities involve playing in squads, the participants learn cooperation and discover the essence of healthy competition among peers. Groups are a platform for exchanging thoughts among the members, which boosts confidence to speak in front of the public and assists in developing the ability to put ideas across others. They get the opportunity to observe and understand the shortcomings and strengths of their contemporaries. Furthermore, children playing as a team acquire significant life lessons such as leadership, sacrifice, compassion, and discipline.

On the contrary, kids who pursue solitary interests are always more confident in making independent decisions. They learn to navigate through complex circumstances without relying on help from others, which enhances their mental faculties to respond swiftly. Children who don't work within groups have better self-understanding. Therefore, this makes them mature enough to take responsibility for their actions.

I reckon the group activities are conducive to children's holistic mental and physical development. They gain several attributes while participating in groups, which are prerequisites to achieving personal growth in different spheres of life.

A child must pursue the activity from which they derive enjoyment during idle time. As a man is a social animal, parents must strive to encourage kids to indulge in team events.

256 Words

Vocab for Task – 13

1. wards – children
2. interpersonal – social
3. persuade – convince
4. uptake - back answer
5. competencies - ability
6. rely – depend
7. essence – significance
8. peers – generation
9. shortcomings – drawbacks
10. contemporaries – colleagues
11. acquire – obtain
12. significant – important
13. compassion – empathy
14. pursue – go after
15. solitary – alone
16. navigate – guide
17. complex – complicated
18. relying – depending
19. enhances – improves
20. faculties – teachers or staff
21. swiftly – very fast
22. conducive – helpful
23. holistic – complete
24. attributes – description
25. prerequisites – necessary
26. spheres – areas
27. derive – originate
28. idle – free
29. strive – aim

TASK 14

These days many people are copying famous celebrities from TV and magazines. Why is this happening? Do you think it is a good idea to copy celebrities?

Media is a mighty tool of modern technology, which has the power to influence the masses at large. The impact of television and magazines is evident in our lives as most people these days are trying to imitate the lifestyle of their favourite stars.

The phenomenon of copying celebrities has only gained popularity recently, and it is more prevalent among the younger generation. Since millennials are born in a time where they have limited possibilities for good role models, they are only able to associate themselves with fictional characters. Celebrities are often depicted on and off-screen as larger-than-life characters, having thrilling activities and only the finest luxuries in life. Consequently, followers are mesmerised by the superficial portrayal of the lifestyle of their icons, and they try to replicate their personalities to escape the harsh realities of life. The inclination towards emulating celebrities is proving to be harmful among young children.

Generally, the lead actors of movies or television programs on-screen commit violence or indulge in sexual performances. Therefore, these depictions can have numerous damaging effects on the impressionable minds of kids. On most occasions, megastars are shown as smoking and consuming alcohol and may promote unhealthy habits and influence youngsters to take up such behaviours. Delinquent conduct of superstars on-screen also leaves a lasting impact on the minds of individuals, which can increase criminal behaviour among citizens.

I reckon society should refrain from idolising fictional heroes. Thus, we must educate the public to appreciate heroes who have made efforts to bring positive changes in themselves and the people around them.

260 Words

Vocab for Task – 14

1. mighty – powerful
2. evident – clear
3. imitate – pretend to be
4. prevalent – widespread
5. millennials – someone between 25-40 years old
6. depicted – described
7. mesmerised – fascinated
8. superficial – artificial
9. portrayal – depiction
10. replicate – copy
11. harsh – rude
12. inclination – tendency
13. emulating – following
14. depictions – description
15. impressionable – easily influenced
16. delinquent – irresponsible
17. lasting – enduring
18. refrain – stop
19. idolizing - adoring

TASK 15

Some people think that formal education should start for children as early as possible. While others think that it should not start until 7 years of age. Discuss both views and give your opinion.

In this day and age, to prepare kids for a highly competitive environment, parents prefer their kids to start formal education as soon as possible. However, some parents do not enrol children in a standard schooling environment before seven.

The decision to not start formal education before the age of seven has its reasons in various scientific studies conducted by scientists. Children usually develop all the essential brain modalities around the age of seven. Therefore, children learn complex lessons more quickly and efficiently than three-year-olds. Delaying formal education until the age of seven gives ample opportunity to teachers and parents to instruct kids with moral education from an early age. Knowledge of morals inspires children to become better human beings who will excel in their personal and professional lives.

On the contrary, with every passing day, competition in education and the job sector is increasing. Consequently, people are leaning towards preparing their kids for the practical world as soon as possible. It is well-established that students have better analytical skills if their formal education begins at three. However, this group is prone to committing trivial errors; and is less physically developed.

I reckon, for the holistic development of children, formal education must not start before the age of seven as it allows all the functions of a child's brain to develop entirely. Students get more time to absorb moral instructions to become better humans.

Before imparting formal education, we must lay a foundation of ethical knowledge in children's life. It will ensure future kids will be good professionals and sincere citizens.

261 Words

Vocab for Task – 15

1. enrol – accept
2. modalities – approach / mood / sensory system
3. efficiently – competently
4. delaying – postponing
5. ample – abundant
6. excel – outdo
7. leaning – tendency
8. analytical – examining
9. prone – likely
10. trivial – not important
11. absorb – taking in information
12. imparting – giving
13. ethical – moral
14. sincere – honest

TASK 16

It is necessary for the parents to attend a parenting training course to bring their children up. Do you agree or disagree?

In this day and age, while nurturing children, parents are facing complex challenges which were unheard of by their previous generations. Thus, it becomes mandatory to learn about children's psychology in the light of the present era through various parenting classes for a better upbringing of the kids.

The majority of people live in nuclear families these days. Consequently, first-time parents often struggle and wander to take proper care of their offspring without the guidance of old and experienced parents. This inclination has given rise to numerous programs focused on imparting essential techniques and skills to perplexed parents who are new to childcare. Training courses usually aim to provide knowledge of the basics of parenting as well as teaching advanced techniques to handle children's tantrums. Furthermore, the unabated exposure of young kids to modern technologies such as media, the internet, and mobile has added more intricacies to already existing traditional difficulties in fostering them. Therefore, these programs help individuals to understand the behaviour of kids at different stages of life and empower them to assist children through their issues.

Additionally, as these courses have years of practical research, parents find these classes very resourceful. These classes enrich parents with vital information to address the issues involved in child-care. Besides, these classes are in groups which allows parents to forge friendships. Friendship among parents helps them to navigate the journey of parenting by learning from the struggles and mistakes of each other.

I reckon, for parents, it has become an absolute prerequisite to undergo parenting classes for the holistic development of their children based on advanced scientific innovations.

267 Words

Vocab for Task – 16

1. nurturing – fostering 9
2. unheard – silent
3. mandatory – compulsory
4. era – time period in history
5. wander – move aimlessly
6. offspring – child
7. inclination – tendency
8. perplexed – confused
9. tantrums – outburst
10. unabated – nonstop
11. exposure – uncovering
12. intricacies – complications
13. fostering – adoption
14. empower – enable
15. resourceful – capable
16. enrich – improve
17. forge – develop / make
18. navigate – guide
19. prerequisite – necessary
20. undergo – experience / feel

TASK 17

Nowadays adults do little exercise. Some people believe that the best way to address this issue is by covering great sporting events such as the Olympics on Television. Others think that it is more beneficial to take other measures. What is your opinion?

In this day and age, the problem that is threatening the health of people across the globe is diseases arising out of a sedentary lifestyle. Numerous government bodies promote active living by telecasting various athletic events on television. However, these steps are falling short, and a more drastic approach is required to check this crisis.

Our focus must be on broadcasting direct information on the advantages of leading a proactive lifestyle rather than covering sporting events to promote workouts. The media outlets must run awareness campaigns disseminating information on welfare policies introduced by the administrations to promote healthy living. Providing incentives in payments of health or life insurance for people living an active lifestyle the government can be a positive step. Since I am committed to achieving a minimum of 8,000 walking steps per day as mandated by the 'World Health Organisation' to live a healthy life in Canada, my health insurance premium is lower than other adults in my household.

Politicians everywhere must endeavour to withdraw taxes on gymnasiums, swimming pools, and fitness equipment to stimulate physical activity among the masses. Contrastingly, enormous events such as Olympics or football world cups have greater reach than any other events in media. These events can inspire young children and others to take up sports and follow a sustainable lifestyle.

With the flooding of sports channels, adults have become couch potatoes, and sports coverage has not yielded the results our policymakers expected. These networks have failed to inculcate an active routine in grown-ups.

I reckon that the events on television cannot make its audience give up their lazy life. Instead, authorities must focus on more practical and dynamic solutions for better outcomes.

280 Words

Vocab for Task – 17

1. sedentary – inactive
2. drastic – extreme
3. crisis – critical condition
4. proactive – energetic
5. disseminating – spreading
6. incentive – encouragement
7. mandate – order / command
8. endeavour - attempt
9. stimulate - inspire
10. enormous - huge
11. sustainable - viable
12. flooding – overflowing / excess of water
13. couch potato – inactive / lazy person
14. yielded - output
15. policy makers - administrators
16. inculcate – instruct
17. dynamic – lively / active

TASK 18

In some cultures, older people are valued most highly. In other cultures, youth is valued more than the experienced. Discuss both views and give your opinion as to which age should be more valued.

There is no denying the fact that experience has no shortcuts. Similarly, the vigour of youth is indeed irreplaceable. However, both stages of life cannot exist without each other.

Across the globe, most communities believe that wisdom comes with age and experience. With the greying of hair, the human mind develops the facilities required to subdue tense situations with patience and diplomacy. I have experienced in my personal and professional life that with the advancement of my age, my capacity to work for long durations has reduced. Nevertheless, my cognitive skills have improved significantly, which helps me to resolve complex circumstances effectively and efficiently. Therefore, it is common for Fortune 500 companies, political parties, and crucial organisations to be under the guidance of people above the age of sixty as aged people command respect easily through their varied skillsets.

Contrastingly when I was young, I had more inclination to take risks while making life-defining decisions. Thus, some societies encourage young generations to take leading roles in significant spheres of life. Dynamic innovations in the contemporary world bring forth a new challenge each day. At the moment, the constant up-gradation of knowledge is a prerequisite to success, which young minds effortlessly can comprehend.

The old and young population have their importance and are an indispensable part of society. I reckon our elders must be valued more than the young population as there are no shortcuts to life experiences and wisdom.

Distinct cultures may view the young and old through their prism of needs and requirements. The majority of cultures, including my indigenous culture, regard elders highly and treat them as our mentors in the path of life and consider it the duty of young children to respect elders.

287 Words

Vocab for Task - 18

1. Vigour - energy
2. Irreplaceable - unique
3. Exist - survive
4. Wisdom - knowledge
5. Subdue – calm
6. Cognitive – mental / intellectual
7. Significantly - importantly
8. Resolve – resolution / determination
9. Contrastingly - in comparison to
10. Inclination – leaning
11. Spheres – areas
12. Dynamic - lively
13. Contemporary - modern
14. Forth - forward
15. Prerequisite - essential
16. Comprehend – understand
17. Indispensable - important
18. Distinct - different

TASK 19

Nowadays celebrities earn more money than politicians. What are the reasons for this? Is it a positive or negative development?

During the last decade, the entertainment industry has seen an enormous rise in revenues as the media's reach is evolving widely. Therefore, it has generated higher incomes for its members. However, politicians earn a small percentage of the earnings of celebrities, which dissuades individuals from taking up politics as a full-time career.

The rapid advancement of technology has made it possible for the media to make inroads into every corner of the world. The development of multi-screen cinemas, online live-streaming platforms, and mobile entertainment applications have broadened the viewership and added new sources of profits. Thus, it has translated into a multi-fold increase in remuneration paid to actors and other personalities.

Politics is not perceived as a commercial space and is perceived as a medium to serve fellow humans. The politicians do not get a salary but an honorarium from the state's exchequer, which usually covers their expenses partially. Besides, political parties have limited opportunities for earnings, as they depend on donations from the public and cannot compensate their politicians for services.

Since representatives of the people perform moral and civil duties under the Constitution of a nation, they must be compensated significantly for their selfless occupation. The unfortunate trend of politicians earning less than celebrities can encourage people to indulge in corruption, which can cause political unrest in a country. Low salaries can deter marginalised communities from participating in democracy. Consequently, it will result in little representation of their demands and oppression at the hands of the majority.

It is an indisputable fact that the remuneration of stars is higher than politicians due to various financial and societal factors. However, fair compensation must be awarded to legislators to appreciate their service to the welfare of society and to curtail its adverse effects.

293 Words

Vocab for Task – 19

1. Enormous - huge
2. Revenues - income
3. Evolving - maturing
4. dissuade - discourages
5. Rapid - fast
6. Inroads – something being encroached
7. Translated - converted
8. Multi-fold - multiple
9. Remuneration - salary
10. Perceived – apparent
11. Honorarium – compensation fee
12. Exchequer – treasury / government fund
13. Compensate - reimburse
14. Unrest - instability
15. Deter - discourage
16. Marginalised - differentiated
17. Oppression - hardship
18. Indisputable - unarguable
19. Appreciate – be grateful
20. Curtail - restrict
21. Adverse - bad

TASK 20

Many people find it difficult to speak in front of and to present to an audience. It is believed that this skill should be taught in school. Why is this important? To what extent do you agree or disagree with it?

Public speaking skills are a significant part of an individual's personality in their personal and professional spheres. However, due to limited opportunities during schooling, most people cannot express their thoughts systematically before an audience.

Generally, fear of public speaking is due to the lack of confidence in presentation skills and the absence of command over the language. People are afraid of not getting the attention of the listeners or speaking incorrectly. These are the outcomes of our education policies, which focus on instructing only theoretical knowledge in schools. Thus, children remain inexperienced in the capabilities required for the practical world.

Nevertheless, techniques of interaction and demonstration must become a substantial part of the academic curriculum. Since these abilities require organic growth, our schooling format must educate students with the aptitude from a tender age. The public speaking instils the confidence to take up leadership roles, which will pave the road for a brighter future for the nation.

The eminence of public speaking skills is evident from the fact that in our lives, the level of education is no longer a measure of an individual's success. Instead, people evaluate success by the way a person interacts with them. I always prefer to employ a person in my law firm with better presentation and communication ability than academic performance. Thus, these skills always assist in standing out and obtaining lucrative employment.

Therefore, to prepare our children to be confident and comfortable in speaking and presenting before listeners, we must endeavour to develop an aptitude for speaking during early education for a person's holistic development.

262 Words

Vocab for Task -20

1. Spheres – areas
2. Systematically - methodically
3. Outcomes - result
4. Substantial - considerable
5. Organic - unprocessed
6. Aptitude - ability
7. Tender - soft
8. Instils - puts
9. Pave - cover
10. Eminence - importance
11. Evaluate - assess
12. Assist - help
13. Lucrative – profitable / well-paid
14. Endeavour - effort
15. Holistic - complete

TASK 21

Many people say that movies and TV programs affect us negatively while others say that they are influential and useful media for us. How do movies and TV affect us?

In our contemporary world, it is a fact that the media is one of the most potent tools to influence the masses. However, the point of deliberation is whether it has benefited the public or only affected us adversely?

The media fulfils the purpose of keeping the public entertained and enchanted. It boosts the happiness and morale of people going through difficult times. During the lockdown period of Coronavirus in Canada, the administrations had imposed strict movement control orders. During that period, I watched movies and television programs that assisted me in keeping a positive outlook to navigate through tough times. Besides, cinema and small-screen series include welfare messages, which promote harmony among different sections of societies to help blur the lines of discrimination and inequality. It also spreads information about welfare agendas to sensitise citizens regarding various social evils.

Since the advancement achieved in the broadcasting domain of television programs, media has been successful in making in-roads across the spectrum of the population. It assists in disseminating useful information to the public on a large-scale during times of crisis to deal with pandemics.

Nevertheless, many people get addicted to media which may lead to a sedentary lifestyle affecting their physical and mental health. Generally, megastars are depicted as smoking and consuming alcohol. It promotes unhealthy habits and influences youngsters to assume such behaviours. The delinquent conduct of superstars on-screen also leaves a lasting impact on the minds of individuals.

With a total viewership of more than three billion globally, the dominance of mass media is incomprehensible. Cinema and small screen have more positive effects on the audience as it has served the dual purpose of entertaining and spreading the social message to society.

285 Words

Vocab for Task – 21

1. Contemporary - modern
2. Patent - copyright
3. Deliberation – thought / discussion
4. Adversely - badly
5. Enchanted – enthralled
6. Morale – confidence / self-esteem
7. Imposed - forced
8. Outlook – viewpoint
9. Navigate - guide
10. Welfare - benefit
11. Harmony – accord
12. Blur – not clear
13. Discrimination - bias
14. Inequality – not equal
15. Agendas - motives
16. Sensitive - delicate
17. Evils - bad
18. Domain - area
19. Spectrum - range
20. Disseminating – broadcasting
21. Sedentary - inactive
22. Depicted - portrayed
23. Delinquent - criminal
24. Incomprehensible – beyond your understanding

TASK 22

Some people think that spending a lot on holding wedding parties, birthday parties and other celebrations is just a waste of money. Others, however, think that these are necessary for individuals and the society. Discuss.

From time immemorial, to express joy, huge expenditures on celebrations are incurred by individuals. The spending spree on a party tax heavily on public and individual resources.

Various natural resources such as food, water and wood are required to arrange the parties. Therefore, we must celebrate on a small scale to preserve natural assets belonging to society and future generations. In most arrangements, eating items are prepared in large quantities. Unfortunately, unconsumed food items are huge waste and loss to the environment and humanity. Extravagant spending also results in endorsing the feeling of envy among different classes of the community and putting people under pressure to arrange events up to the standards of their contemporaries by spending more capital than they can afford. In some cultures, people are subject to the societal stigma of incapacity to spend generously on social events.

Contrastingly, observing celebrations is a way to express pleasure moments in the life of individuals and a way to stay connected with extended family members. Festivities are significant to preserve our old cultures as these are the perfect stage to introduce family traditions to the younger generation.

From the perspective of society at large, it is a path to inclusiveness by embracing other members of society in times of happiness. Therefore, it propagates harmony and brings communities closer by blurring the lines of differences. It is a path to inclusiveness by embracing other members of society in your times of happiness.

Celebrating a life event is a substantial part of human life and culture. Nevertheless, hefty expenditures on events that last only for short moments are unnecessary and do not benefit society or individuals.

275 Words

Vocab for Task – 22

1. Immemorial - ancient
2. Incurred – suffered
3. Spree – binge / splurge
4. Taxes – duties / levies
5. Assets - possessions
6. Extravagant - excessive
7. Endorsing – advertising
8. Envy - jealousy
9. Contemporaries - generation
10. Stigma – shame / disgrace
11. Incapacity - inability
12. Generously - kindly
13. Inclusiveness - completeness
14. Embracing - reaching
15. Propagates - spread
16. Blurring – distorting / confusing
17. Substantial - large
18. Hefty - heavy

TASK 23

Many people say that the only way to guarantee a good job is to complete a course of university education. Others claim that it is better to start work after school and gain experience in the world of work. Discuss

Generally, people believe the only way to find a lucrative job is through formal education. However, people are breaking away from the traditional school of thought. Many individuals prefer a job after completing high school to gain practical experience these days.

Working at an early age under a senior allows the new entrant to gain trade secrets and acquire experience under his guidance. The future of young employees becomes brighter as they have a chance to learn technicalities of the trade from an experienced person and can quickly rise in ranks through their performance-oriented approach. In my teens, I started working at a computer repair shop and developed a keen interest in technology. After completing high school, a leading computer hardware company engaged me as a technician, based on my practical knowledge and the recommendation of my mentors.

Contrastingly, some occupations may require a mandatory university degree or certificate, becoming a hindrance to getting the desired job. The post-secondary education equips the student with the necessary confidence and self-esteem to compete in the job market. Thus, they earn higher than people with high school diplomas.

I can personally endorse the view that formal education has little or no bearing on finding a white-collar job. If a person is passionate about their work, people can work up to the higher ranks in an organisation.

A degree from a university may or may not help in gaining employment. However, the most advantageous way to a job is to begin working early in life since there are no shortcuts to experience.

258 Words

Vocab for Task – 23

1. Lucrative - profitable
2. Entrant - applicant
3. Oriented - focussed
4. Mandatory - compulsory
5. Hindrance – obstacle / difficulty
6. Equips - contains
7. Endorse - promote
8. Bearing – contribution

TASK 24

More and more companies are allowing employees to work at home. Do you think this is a positive or negative development?

During the past decade, rapid technological innovations have permitted organisations to encourage their staff to work remotely. This trend has boosted productivity and provided much-needed freedom from rigid working hours.

The recent 'Coronavirus' pandemic has forced most companies across the globe to allow their workers to perform their duties from their homes. This development has been beneficial to both employees as well as employers. The work-from-home model provides a comfortable environment for the personnel, which is very conducive for people performing high-concentration jobs. The traditional eight-hour working time frame from 9 to 5 has become obsolete in the era of globalisation. Therefore, freedom to employees from a schedule allows them to maintain an equilibrium between family and work life.

Besides, the option to work from home is now a significant factor when selecting a prospective job by highly skilled people. During the pandemic, my organisation asked me to work from home. Even after the pandemic, I have opted to work from home since I am more satisfied with my profession by achieving targets on time, which has positively affected my personal life with the family.

The drawback of this model is the lack of physical communication and decaying of interpersonal relationships between co-workers, which hurts teamwork. Since the employee is in a home environment, distractions, and lack of supervision lead to less productivity.

The work-from-home job system has become a necessity for businesses rather than an alternative. I reckon performing job responsibilities as per the work from the home model has various positive impacts on all the parties.

258 Words

Vocab for Task – 24

1. Remotely – from a distance
2. Boosted - backed
3. Rigid - strong
4. Conducive - favourable
5. Obsolete – out of date
6. Equilibrium - balance
7. Prospective – point of view
8. Opted - choose
9. Decaying - rotten
10. Interpersonal – social / between persons

TASK 25

More and More pollution and waste are created nowadays. What are the problems caused by this? What solutions can be provided to solve these problems?

Across the globe, to satisfy the necessities of the exploding population, large-scale mining and production of resources are taking place. As a result, these activities harm the environment in numerous ways, which have become a modern-day epidemic.

Numerous human actions emanated pollution and waste, which is the cause of the degradation of our habitat. The extraction of minerals, mass production of plastic items, and vehicular pollution are the leading causes. The rising temperature of the earth due to the release of greenhouse gases into our atmosphere is a direct cause of pollution and waste generated by humans.

Global warming is a leading cause of rising water levels, which may submerge many island nations and states into the sea in the coming years. The ecological balance has been disturbed due to deforestation to create wastelands, which led to the extinction of many rare animal and plant species. Furthermore, chronic ailments of the lungs, eyes, and skin are common these days due to pollutants emitted from factories and vehicles.

Governments and individuals around the globe are taking cautious steps to check the escalating pollution and waste. Recycling materials and sorting wet and dry waste at their source can reduce waste significantly, which otherwise would be dumped into landfills untreated. Moreover, special highway lanes dedicated to carpooling can encourage people to travel by private vehicles. Besides, individuals should use non-renewable resources carefully and refrain from using pollutants such as single-use plastic.

To stop the deterioration of the atmosphere from pollution, everyone must pledge to use natural assets collectively and judicially. If all countries cooperate, this will ensure less pollution and waste for the betterment of the coming generations.

275 Words

Vocab for Task – 25

1. Epidemic – widespread
2. Emanated – originate
3. Submerge – immerse
4. Chronic – long-lasting
5. Ailments – illnesses
6. Sorting – categorisation
7. Deterioration – worsening
8. Judicially – sensibly

TASK 26

Some people think medical knowledge is the most important skill that nurses should have. Others believe there are other more important qualities. Discuss both views and give your opinion.

Professional nurses require specialised skills and undergo numerous years of tedious medical study and training. However, a few individuals have continued to argue that a medical attendant needs more than bookish knowledge. They state that nurses must possess qualities such as empathy and benevolence to be successful in this field.

Across the globe, to uphold the quality of professionals and to maintain the standards of services, every job requires its entrants to acquire basic academic knowledge to profess the profession. Nurses without medical information cannot profess occupation and control complex situations involving human life. Unfamiliarity with the subject is detrimental to a patient's health. Moreover, it will expose nurses to various unknown on-job medical hazards, which may be prejudicial to their lives.

In addition to clinical information, nurses must be able to form an emotional bond with their patients as it helps in taking care of the person more diligently. Sometimes, patients respond positively to emotional touch rather than therapeutic protocols while recovering from post-traumatic injuries. Medical assistants spend most of their time caring for patients undergoing mental and physical agony. Thus, having compassion for patients assists nurses in effectively performing their jobs.

Since nurses work alongside doctors round the clock, they need advanced medical information instead of other qualities to comprehend technical terms used during medical procedures and efficiently officiate their duties.

As nurses are first responders to emergencies, it is paramount that they must be well-versed with medical knowledge more than other skills to deal with the situation and patients successfully.

253 Words

Vocab for Task – 26

1. Undergo - experience
2. Tedious - boring
3. Possess - own
4. Empathy - understanding
5. Benevolence - kindness
6. Entrants - applicants
7. Profess - admit
8. Unfamiliarity – strangeness
9. Detrimental – harmful
10. Hazard - danger
11. Diligently - carefully
12. Therapeutic - healing
13. Protocol - procedure
14. Traumatic – shocking / disturbing
15. Agony – anguish / pain
16. Compassion - sympathy
17. Round the clock – nonstop
18. Comprehend - understand
19. Officiate - manage
20. Responders – first reactors
21. Paramount - supreme
22. Well-versed - familiar

TASK 27

Some people think that school children should be asked to work individually in class. Others believe that working in small groups is better. Discuss both views and give your opinion.

The learning acquired at the school level prepares children for their future professional and personal lives. Throughout schooling, various assignments are awarded to children, which they are required to accomplish independently and in groups.

Most parents believe that children must work in groups as it inculcates life-long etiquette of sharing and other soft skills, which help them become better human beings. The kids assimilate qualities such as selflessness and empathy while performing in a union. They acquire the knowledge of difficulties faced during the completion of various tasks by their peers, which expands their emotional and mental horizons. Hence, children become socially aware and forge friendships. They learn how to express themselves to an audience and build public speaking skills required for future leadership roles. Furthermore, students learn the significance of the team spirit needed to succeed and complete the task at hand while working alongside their contemporaries.

Contrastingly, if students perform individually, their abilities will be appreciated more when they complete work without the support of a team. Besides, the examinations are designed in a way to test the intelligence of an individual. Therefore, children must be encouraged to work alone to develop the aptitude to overcome obstacles without outside aid. Moreover, autonomous decisions assist in developing the habit of taking responsibility for all the outcomes, whether positive or negative.

I reckon, given the holistic advancement of our children, we must encourage them to work in small groups. Working in teams allows students to learn while enjoying the school experience in the company of their friends.

257 Words

Vocab for Task – 27

1. Inculcates – teaches / instructs
2. Etiquette - manners
3. Assimilate – adapt
4. Empathy - understanding
5. Unions – amalgamations / mergers
6. Peers – friends / colleagues
7. Horizon – prospect
8. Forge – make / develop
9. Contemporaries – colleagues
10. Aptitude - skill
11. Obstacles - difficulties
12. Autonomous - independent
13. Outcomes - results

TASK 28

Some people believe that successful sports teams are always those with the strongest or fittest players. Others think that success depends more on the team's mental strength. Discuss both views and give your own opinion.

Teams involved in sports undergo numerous years of tedious physical and mental training. Many people incline towards the thought that the fittest teams have better chances of winning. Yet, teams with higher mental conditioning are outperforming physically strong teams.

Players go to extreme lengths to prepare themselves mentally to survive a ruthless sporting environment. Often, groups of players having higher mental conditioning triumph over physically fit teams during high-pressure games. The glaring example I witnessed was in Auckland during the rugby world cup of 2011. In that event, New Zealand's rugby team used to perform a traditional dance called 'Maori Dance' before every game. The dance moves were aggressive and loud, charging the local audience and creating mental pressure on the opposition. The 'Kiwi' squad was not the strongest among other nations. Yet, their strategy was successful in winning the tournament.

In contrast, sports stars having brute power and physical capabilities have lesser chances of incurring injuries during close-contact events such as football and basketball. Hence, it allows them to play throughout long sporting tournaments without fearing harm to their significant members. Furthermore, groups that emphasise physical training can intimidate competitors through their sheer physical appearance to negatively affect the mental state of the opposite team.

Undeniably, across sports, teams undertake excruciating physical and mental conditioning. I reckon squads having robust psychological capabilities is more likely to be professionally successful as they have higher chances of success under pressure situations.

Since the participants of various sports have become thorough professionals, it has given rise to cut-throat competition in all sporting events. The teams without fit players cannot survive the games, but to win the occasions, they require higher mental power.

280 Words

Vocab for Task – 28

1. Tedious - dull
2. Outperforming - exceeding
3. Ruthless - cruel
4. Triumph - success
5. Glaring - obvious
6. Emphasize - stress
7. Incurring - acquiring
8. brute - beast
9. intimidate - threaten
10. sheer - total
11. undeniably - unquestionably
12. excruciating - unbearable
13. robust - strong

TASK 29

Some people say it is a good idea for all employees to wear a uniform at work.
To what extent do you agree or disagree?

With the inception of roles and designations at work, the uniform has become an integral part of all organisations to define responsibilities. I resonate with the statement that uniforms must be a fundamental element of an employee's personality at the job.

Whether businesses are small, medium or large, they have a basic form of attire, which is mandatory for their workers to wear on the job. Most professions maintain the highest degree of discipline and equality with the help of a standard dress code. The significance of uniforms is evident from a person wearing similar clothes developing a sense of belongingness and oneness with co-workers. Besides, the difference in uniforms assists the outsiders and internal parties to differentiate various roles of people in a workplace, eliminating any confusion while dealing with the concerned person.

Additionally, people wearing clothes bearing signage of a prestigious company tend to develop positive psychological traits such as pride and confidence. Thus, it instils confidence to tackle complex situations and fills them with satisfaction to work for an esteemed company.

Sometimes uniforms may pose a hindrance to the productivity of the employees as uniforms suppress the individuality of the person. Uncomfortable or unattractive uniforms reduce enthusiasm and lead to inefficient performances. Furthermore, the expenditure on maintenance can be a prominent issue for employees as well as the employers.

There are several merits attached to having a uniform at the workplace. Therefore, every office must strive to follow a dress code. Nevertheless, we must not impose uniforms and must prepare in consultation and participation from the workers, which will increase their confidence and comfort.

267 Words

Vocab for Task -29

1. inception - start
2. resonate – echo / reverberate
3. mandatory - compulsory
4. eliminating – getting rid of
5. bearing - tolerating
6. prestigious - esteemed
7. instils – put in
8. esteemed - impressive
9. pose - cause
10. hindrance - obstacle
11. prominent - famous
12. strive - attempt
13. impose - force

TASK 30

Some people think that job satisfaction is the most important factor when looking for a job. Others think that having job security is more important. Discuss both views and give your own opinion.

During the last decade, the literacy rate has soared tremendously, resulting in cut-throat competition for each job position. It has propelled people to choose job security over job satisfaction while looking for employment.

The foremost reason for an individual to be engaged in a career he or she is passionate about is that they can perform duties without feeling stressed and enjoy the efforts involved in officiating responsibilities. The outcomes will be more effective, and a person can experience more pleasure and recognition in his professional life. When people derive satisfaction from their occupation, they are more likely to succeed swiftly than their co-workers. All these encouraging factors uplift confidence and self-esteem, having a positive impact on personal life.

On the contrary, job security is now a primary factor for many people as the market has become volatile due to fears of retrenchment. Most job seekers demand security in their employment. Accordingly, most prospective job seekers are inclined to seek a sense of security in their occupation as it gives them financial autonomy and mental peace to perform their duties without pressure.

I reckon that no level of job security can quench the need for job satisfaction. Only Job satisfaction can bring effectiveness and happiness in one's personal and professional life. Hence, it must be the most significant factor while searching for employment.

People usually do not have the freedom to select jobs as per their satisfaction because of shrinking employment opportunities. Nevertheless, some people still prefer to work in a profession where they feel contented.

256 Words

Vocab for Task – 30

1. soared - rise
2. tremendously - extremely
3. propelled - forced
4. derive - obtain
5. volatile - unstable
6. retrenchment - cutback
7. prospective – point of view
8. inclined - bent
9. autonomy - independence
10. quench - satisfy
11. shrinking – lessening
12. contended - satisfied

TASK 31

There is less communication between family members today than in the past. Do you agree or disagree?

In yesteryears, families used to be closed-knit units, and communication between members was free flow. However, this trend has taken a significant downshift with the introduction of technological innovations, which resulted in people spending less time with their family members.

The new generation spends more time on social media, online gaming, and virtual reality applications, which causes a rift in relationships as people have fewer interactions with loved ones. Over the past decade, technology has negatively impacted the behaviour of youngsters as they are more aggressive and detach themselves from close relationships. The youngest generation and millennials are more inclined towards communicating through various virtual means rather than meeting in person, even in their intimate affairs. The transformation in the family structure from joint family to nuclear is another factor in creating spaces within family members in contrast to the past eras.

The cut-throat competition in the job market mandates an individual to put in long working hours, which does not allow people to spend quality time together and maintain equilibrium between work and family. Since several people are migrating to foreign countries in search of better avenues, families are unable to meet with each other for longer times. Families get drift due to long distances and lack of communication opportunities.

It is undisputed that the communication between family members is declining. Nevertheless, to preserve the social fabric of our family system, we must encourage open communication between all the family members to diminish the self-created distance between different age groups.

251 Words

Vocab for Task – 31

1. yesteryears - past
2. rift - gap
3. interaction - communication
4. detach - separate
5. millennial – people in age group 25-40
6. intimate - close
7. mandates – directives
8. equilibrium - balance
9. avenues – paths
10. undisputed - certain
11. fabric - material
12. diminish - reduce

TASK 32

Mobile phones and the Internet are used by millions of people every day, but old people use these forms of technology the least. In what ways can mobile phones and the Internet be helpful for older people? What measures can be taken to encourage older people to use them more?

In this day and age, technology has integrated into the human lifestyle. Nobody is unfamiliar with its uses and advantages. However, the ratio of the old generation using modern creations is way less than young people.

Due to the lack of awareness in older folks, they fail to actualise the true potential of modern know-how. Elders unable to cope-up with the swift changes in technology resist adopting it. Besides, they are uninformed about technical terms and lack knowledge of the complex steps involved.

The foremost advantage of knowing about technology can be monitoring and resolving health issues through gadgets like heart rate monitors, health bands, and telemedicine. Since seniors can seek consultancy from numerous specialists online with the aid of mobile and the internet, they are not required to leave the comfort of their homes and risk their health by visiting hospitals and clinics. All the necessities such as medicines and groceries are available at the swipe of a fingertip, which can be particularly helpful to people living alone without any assistance. Besides, technology is a significant source of entertainment and learning, which keeps the brain engaged and attentive.

To empower elders, administrations should organise workshops to impart basic knowledge of technology at retirement homes and senior citizen's clubs. Through the aid of welfare legislation, it can be obligatory for manufacturers to make mobile phones user-friendly for seniors, which will help them to adopt the technology without reservations.

Technology is significant for bringing a revolution to the lives of our older generation regarding their health, safety, and entertainment. Therefore, we must encourage and educate them to accept technology and use it to improve their quality of life.

277 Words

Vocab for Task-32

1. integrated - included
2. unfamiliar - unknown
3. swift - fast
4. Actualise – realise
5. know-how - knowledge
6. resist - oppose
7. assistance - support
8. engaged - occupied
9. attentive - alert
10. empower – authorise
11. impart - give
12. legislation – law of government
13. obligatory - mandatory
14. reservations – doubts

TASK 33

In some countries, people waste a lot of the food that they buy in shops and restaurants. Why do you think this is? What can be done to solve this problem?

The problem of wasteful consumables purchased at shops or restaurants arises due to an individual's insensitive buying behaviour and ignorance toward our limited natural assets.

The foremost cause of food wastage is people tend to purchase quantities more than their actual requirements. The excess either goes uneaten or gets spoiled. Across the globe, in developed economies, consumers have high disposable income, and food items are obtainable in surplus as the productivity rate is high. Thus, people are more prone to obtaining extra groceries or meals at a restaurant than they need. Marketing campaigns or promotions such as 'buy one get one, persuade people to buy more than their consumption capacity.

People residing in countries with higher agricultural production have less empathy towards the misapplication of food as surplus eatables are available at throwaway prices. Furthermore, in contemporary social media life, to maintain their influence and status, people order a variety of foods to post pictures on social media.

The principal measure to check the wastage of resources must be in the shape of enacting legislation to levy hefty fines on customers leaving unconsumed food on their tables. Besides, the government should focus on developing campaigns to disseminate information on the burden of wasteful practices on the economy and its participants. At the micro-level, individuals can amend their bulk buying patterns and ensure full utilisation of items in their pantry.

I reckon authorities must impose strict restrictions to check unnecessary wastage of food. Moreover, people should consume food judiciously to stop wastage.

251 Words

Vocab for Task- 33

1. squandering – carelessness / reckless
2. excess - overload
3. disposable - throwaway
4. surplus - extra
5. prone - likely
6. persuade - convince
7. misapplication – abuse / misuse
8. throwaway - discard
9. levy - tax
10. hefty - large
11. enacting - passing
12. disseminate - separate
13. amend - modify
14. pantry – storeroom
15. judicious – careful / sensible

TASK 34

In some countries, people prefer to rent a house than buy one. What are the advantages and disadvantages of renting a property?

Since land is a limited resource and with the ever-booming global population, housing prices are increasing astonishingly. Therefore, to ensure financial liberation, most prospective home buyers are leaning towards the option of leasing.

The primary reason people are renting houses is attributed to the ease of process as it is economical as well as straightforward. In metro-politician cities, purchasing a property can be a cumbersome and expensive legal exercise. Renting provides more mobility as a person can live within the predominant location of a city, and that too, without fearing to pay astronomical municipal taxes associated with ownership. Places offered on the rental market are usually fully furnished, therefore, renter does not require to incur expenditure or effort towards setting up a household. Renting is appropriate for people immigrating to a new place or looking for a dwelling option without investing huge sums.

Nevertheless, the tenancy has proved to be a tiresome and expensive experience for renters. If the contract is not renewed, the tenants may require finding and moving into a new house. Tenanted premises do not offer a sense of ownership as the legal impediments restrict the occupant from enjoying the place unfettered. In some countries, not owning a place to live is considered a social stigma, as well as it can affect the standing of a person in the community.

The decision to possess or lease out a unit is grounded in numerous personal, social, and financial circumstances of an individual. However, I reckon, given the astronomical housing prices in the present scenario, it is more advantageous to rent rather than to own a house.

268 Words

Vocab for Task-34

1. Astonishingly - surprisingly
2. Liberation - freedom
3. Prospective – potential
4. Leaning - liking
5. Leasing - hire
6. Attributed - credited
7. Mobility - movement
8. Cumbersome - bulky
9. Predominant - major
10. Incur - earn
11. Dwelling - house
12. Tenancy - occupancy
13. Tiresome - boring
14. Impediment - obstacle
15. Unfettered – unregulated
16. Stigma – disgrace / shame
17. Astronomical – sky-high

TASK 35

Nowadays people are less fit and healthy than they were in the past, which could affect their long-term health. Why do you think this is? What can be done to solve this problem?

The advancement of innovative technologies has reduced the human efforts required for performing routine errands. Consequently, modern people are leading a sedentary lifestyle, which has given rise to complex health issues affecting people throughout their stages of existence.

The foremost factor attributed to deterioration in the general health of humans is following an indiscipline regime. The individuals are sleeping fewer than six hours or have erratic sleep patterns due to the unabated use of mobile phones and computers before going to bed. Thus, people feel lethargic during the daytime, which renders them to miss the exercise to stay fit.

In recent times, people consume more fast food containing higher fatty acids than in the past, which is an underlining reason for obesity and unfit physiques. Furthermore, overweight individuals have higher chances of contracting significant health complications involving heart and liver ailments. Adulterated consumables laced with high-potency fertilisers and dangerous chemicals finding their way into drinking water are other factors contributing to the worsening health crisis.

Administrations must endeavour to check this epidemic by enacting several legislations to curtail harmful emissions into the environment without being treated. The government must educate and disseminate information through campaigns regarding the positive impacts of living a healthy lifestyle. On the micro-level, individuals must strictly adhere to perform the exercise as per daily activity time prescribed by the World Health Organisation for a sustainable way of living.

The fact is indisputable that currently, people are less disease-free than previous generations. Nevertheless, humans must inculcate exercise and healthy eating habits to uplift their well-being.

259 Words

Vocab for Task – 35

1. Errands – odd jobs
2. Sedentary - inactive
3. Attributed - credited
4. Deterioration - worsening
5. Erratic - unreliable
6. Regime - routine
7. Unabated – nonstop
8. Lethargic - lazy
9. Render – cause to be
10. Underlining - attention
11. Adulterated - impure
12. Laced – lined
13. Enacting – endorsing
14. Potency - strength
15. Curtail - restrict
16. Adhere – follow / obey
17. Inculcate – teach / instruct
18. Uplift - raise

TASK 36

Many people think that the most important things in life are free (i.e., they cannot be bought). Do you agree or disagree?

Currently, people attach significance to matters which carry monetary value. They are spending more time gathering the means of enjoyment without realising the fact that valuable things in life are available at no cost.

Feelings such as love, satisfaction, and companionship can be derived naturally at no expense, which ought to be the priorities in life. An individual can spend their whole existence accumulating wealth, yet good health is required, without which a person cannot enjoy worldly possessions. The feeling of eternal happiness cannot be bought in the market and is only achieved through personal satisfaction. Being a Lawyer, I have seen in my professional experience that people in high-income groups are usually less satisfied with their life due to lack of close relationships and more financial disputes. Contrastingly, the zeal for life is higher in the economically weaker sections, thus, I realised important things in life cannot be bought.

Additionally, humans are social beings, which is one of the most important spheres in our relationships. We must respect a good association and endeavour to invest time and efforts in our loved ones. Mother nature has blessed us with natural splendours such as mountains, rivers, and shores, which are a substantial source of entertainment and enjoyment. Nevertheless, the basic necessitates of life such as food, medicine, and housing are not free, and one must work towards acquiring them.

It is an indisputable fact that the majority of people get enticed by worldly achievements and possessions, however, I agree with the statement that the most significant things in life come at no cost.

262 Words

Vocab for Task- 36

1. Monetary - financial
2. Priorities - preferences
3. Derived - obtained
4. Eternal - endless
5. Disputes - fights
6. Zeal - passion
7. Splendour - brilliance
8. Substantial - large
9. Enticed – lured / tempted
10. Indisputable – clear / undeniable

TASK 37

Some sports are extremely dangerous for those who play them. Why do people participate in such sports? What measures could they take to minimise the risks involved?

Since the inception of civilisation, humans have been out to test their physical and mental limits under the most challenging circumstances. These experiments have given rise to the concept of extreme sports, which involves fatal risks for its participants while providing entertainment to its viewers.

Every sport carries some form of risk of injury or life, however, close contact sports or adventure sports like wrestling, car racing or skiing involves higher risk than usual. The primary reason people are obsessed with daredevil sports is the outrageous level of recognition and money that these activities can provide within a short period. Parental pressure in some communities to participate in masculine games may force kids to take up such dangerous games.

A scientific reason why people derive enjoyment from performing daring activities is due to the release of a hormone in the body known as adrenaline. These enzymes, when released, induce feelings of satisfaction and achievement to which the person gets addicted. Consequently, individuals develop a constant need to participate in dangerous games. People accomplishing tasks involving paramount risks become extremely motivated to replicate their performances as well as to improve their previous outcomes to present their abilities to undertake risk.

To avoid fatal eventualities, one must follow all the appropriate measures and adhere sternly to all safety protocols to mitigate risks involved in such sports. Furthermore, sportsmen should operate under the guidance of field experts and must perform after going through proper physical and mental conditioning required as per established standards.

Sports infamous for life-threatening perils are more gratifying and entertaining, nevertheless, keeping in view the well-being of contestants, activities ought to be performed with utmost caution.

276 Words

Vocab for Task- 37

1. Inception - start
2. Fatal - dangerous
3. Obsessed - gripped
4. Outrageous - shameful
5. Derive - obtain
6. Masculine - manly
7. replicate - copy
8. paramount - supreme
9. eventualities - outcomes
10. adhere - listen
11. sternly - severely
12. utmost - extreme
13. caution - carefulness
14. perils - danger
15. gratifying - rewarding

TASK 38

In many countries traditional customs are being lost. Why do you think this is? What can parent and schools do to keep traditional customs alive?

Humans are at the pinnacle in the dimensions of science and innovation. We rely solely on technology in every sphere of our lives, which has resulted in diminished use and significance of customs in everyday life.

The majority has stopped professing ancient traditions as they feel that if tested on the parameters of modern science, they will have no practical standing in their contemporary world. With the change in the lifestyle and generation, most customs are outdated as dressing styles, eating habits, and working manners are swiftly evolving. Many customs or traditions against the parameters of modern human rights have been outlawed by administrations, thereby restricting their usage. Furthermore, shortcomings in the knowledge of applications and the positive impacts of observing customs have resulted in a sharp decline in its popularity in several communities. In South-East Asia, the colonial era's shadow has pressured the population living in commonwealth countries to adhere to the western lifestyle. It has resulted in ignoring their culture and losing cultural identity to foreign superpowers.

Parents must become role models by following all the customs to inculcate them in their children's daily lives. Parents should spend time with children to educate children regarding the eminence of customs.

In schools, the academic curriculum must incorporate information about the history and the significance of observing customs. Children must be encouraged to participate in tours of museums and customary sites to examine various traditions.

Drastic measures are necessary to promote traditional customs, as culture is the invisible bond that ties an individual to one's language, identity, and individuality.

Or

Culture is the invisible bond that ties an individual to language, identity, and individuality. Hence, drastic measures are necessary to promote and preserve traditional customs.

259 Words

Vocab for Task- 38

1. pinnacle - peak
2. rely - depend
3. solely - completely
4. dimensions - size
5. professing – owning
6. swiftly - fast
7. evolving – budding / developing
8. inculcate – teach / instruct
9. eminence – famed / renowned
10. incorporate – add in / include
11. drastic - extreme
12. invisible – unseen

TASK 39

Some people believe that all students should be made to have an unpaid job in their free time. Do you agree or disagree?

In this day and age, parents plan their children's routines to the last hour of the day to utilise idle time for productive activities. Some believe that students must perform voluntary jobs to learn and hone life skills during their leisure period.

The unpaid jobs can provide a much-required platform for youngsters to showcase their talents without having the pressure of outcomes. Since the children are seated under the guidance of industry experts, they have an opportunity to enhance their existing abilities and forge relationships to help them in future. In an apprenticeship program, kids can discover their interests, which can help them to choose their subjects accordingly at school. Thus, it assists them in making an informed decision while deciding on their career paths in the future. During a project in my schooling days, I had an opportunity to work as an unpaid intern in the office of a leading lawyer in the city. The training positively influenced my personality, and I was motivated to perform better in academics to become a lawyer myself.

Many parents and young people think that voluntary services can help develop a wide range of competencies, such as the capacity to assume responsibility, time management, and financial freedom. Besides, an after-school job under adult supervision provides constructive use of free time for teenagers as it is an opportunity to focus on life and leaves them with less time to engage in any delinquency.

I reckon doing unpaid jobs teaches significant traits such as responsibility and work ethic in a youngster, which prepares an individual to face life realities comfortably in the future.

268 Words

Vocab for Task- 39

1. idle - free
2. hone – sharpen / improve
3. voluntary – willing / unpaid
4. apprenticeship – internship / training
5. forge – to make / develop
6. competencies - abilities
7. delinquency - criminal
8. traits - features
9. ethic – moral principle

TASK 40

After finishing school, some students go travelling or work for some time instead of going directly to university. Do you think the advantages of gap years outweigh the disadvantages?

Most people are inclined to enrol in post-secondary education immediately after completing high school as it prepares them for their upcoming professions. However, some students prefer to take a sabbatical to gain practical experience in the real world before joining regular studies at the university level.

The gap years are helpful to recreate as well as explore various interests by travelling or working. This opportunity gives students ample time to self-actualise to make their future academic choices through a fresh perspective. Experiences learned while at job or globetrotting can be channelled to select a suitable career resonating with an individual's abilities. Additionally, the time invested in co-curricular activities during this period can contribute to gaining valuable life skills to handle complex situations through time and financial management. Since higher studies have astronomical fee structures, students can save money to finance their education by working on jobs and attaining monetary liberty.

Nevertheless, taking a gap year in some societies is frowned upon and may be considered neglect as it does not conform to community norms. The stigma of a gap may negatively affect the confidence and academic performance of the student. After a gap period, the process of integrating with studies is not as smooth as it may seem for most students. They may face difficulty adapting to the excruciating study regimes required by institutes of higher education.

Break years between two educational institutions can be beneficial, however, the decision depends on one's personal choice. I reckon sometimes we must step back to leap forward as the enumerated merits of gap periods triumph its drawbacks.

264 Words

Vocab for Task- 40

1. inclines - bent
2. enrol - admit
3. recreate – build again
4. ample – in abundance
5. perspective – point of view
6. globetrotting - tourism
7. channelled - guided
8. resonating – similar to
9. astronomical – sky-high
10. monetary - financial
11. liberty - freedom
12. dereliction - neglect
13. norms - rules
14. stigma - shame
15. integrating - combining
16. excruciating - awful
17. regimes - routine
18. enumerate – several
19. triumph - victory

TASK 41

These days children watch television programs and play computer games, which their friends watch and play. Do you think parents should stop their children to follow their friends?

Across the globe, parents are working towards providing their children with opportunities to take their decisions independently. However, most young kids do not apply their minds and succumb to the pressure of peers while making choices regarding sources of entertainment.

In this day and age, technological innovations like the internet and social media platforms have made inroads into each household, making it convenient for kids to acquire knowledge of the latest trends in gaming and television. The harmful tendency of following contemporaries while consuming mass media content is becoming an impediment to the physical as well as mental growth of kids. Children are not exploring interests or hobbies as per their wishes, which can give them more pleasure. Therefore, when children premise their decisions regarding watching television programs on the liking of their friends, their capability to make autonomous decisions is curtailed.

Additionally, while deciding on the choice of entertainment for kids, the communication regarding the selection is diminishing between children and parents. Kids these days are inclined more towards the preferences of their companions.

Parents must take proactive measures to tackle this sensitive issue with maturity. They must inform children regarding suitable games and shows available for their recreation. They must empower children to make informed decisions while selecting an activity. Besides, students at schools and homes must be taught not to become victims of other people's opinions and passing trends, which may prove unproductive for their future.

Parents must help children to make independent decisions regarding the choice of television programs or other entertainment sources. However, decisions should be without the influence of their friends or parents.

269 Words

Vocab for Task - 41

1. succumb - surrender
2. peers – colleagues
3. convenient – easy to be
4. inroads – being encroached
5. tendency - ability
6. contemporaries – colleagues
7. impediment - obstacle
8. premise - basis
9. autonomous - independent
10. curtailed - restrained
11. diminishing - lessening
12. companions - friends
13. proactive - energetic
14. empower - boost
15. recreation – leisure

TASK 42

Living in a country where you have to speak a foreign language can cause serious social problems, as well as practical problems. To what extent do you agree or disagree with this statement?

Rapid globalisation has resulted in the large-scale migration of human resources. It provides better life opportunities to newcomers in a foreign land. However, they face numerous social and other challenges in their day-to-day lives while adapting to foreign languages.

The foremost issue while using a foreign language can be a lack of a clear understanding of local dialects. One cannot comprehend the local words and slang without spending significant time in a foreign country. Some people may take quite a while to integrate into the new community and may be subject to resistance from its old inhabitants. New immigrants are labelled as outsiders because their speaking style is distinct from natives. Many face discrimination at the hands of society and may feel depressed by non-inclusive behaviour. Since humans always desire to be part of society, one cannot survive in isolation. If an individual cannot communicate properly in a foreign language, acquiring acquaintances becomes difficult, becoming a massive hindrance while adjusting to a new life.

Furthermore, the incapacity to communicate adequately in an alien language will create grave practical problems while searching for employment. Immigrants may have limited job openings as recruiters are inclined to employ native speakers for better communication with clients. Moreover, a simple task such as asking for directions can become daunting if the person does not understand the language properly.

People must achieve advanced writing and speaking skills in the foreign language to integrate smoothly with society and to avoid the most practical and social complications associated with using a different language.

255 Words

Vocab for Task – 42

1. rapid - fast
2. dialect - language
3. comprehend - understand
4. slang – dialect
5. integrate - add
6. resistance - struggle
7. labelled - named
8. distinct - unique
9. natives - citizens
10. hindrance - obstacles
11. acquaintances - links
12. incapacity – inability
13. adequately - sufficiently
14. alien - foreigner
15. grave - serious
16. recruiters - employment agency
17. daunting - boring
18. integrate - mix

TASK 43

Overpopulation of urban areas has led to numerous problems. Identify one or two serious ones and suggest ways by which government and individuals can tackle these problems.

Across the globe, the infrastructure of major cities is reeling under the pressure of a population explosion. Various amenities such as health, transportation, and education are negatively affected by the high number of citizens living in urban areas.

Overpopulation of metros has been caused primarily due to the lack of family planning and little use of contraceptives among the younger generation. The urban inhabitants producing a high level of emissions are contributing to the rapid depletion of the environment. The harmful pollutants across the globe are causing several health problems ranging from skin irritation, breathing difficulties, and auditory issues in most cities.

Besides, a big challenge that administrations are facing right now is to keep up with the outrageous volumes of daily commuters using various public transports within city limits. The deteriorating state of mass transit is forcing individuals to use private vehicles, which leads to traffic snarls and parking troubles.

The government must ensure that people are scattered equally among provinces. This system will lead to the holistic development of all the regions. The new residential and industrial areas within the countryside will assist in easing off the burden on the municipalities. Furthermore, at the micro-levels, individuals must endeavour to reduce their carbon footprint by adhering to recycling and sorting of the waste at the source. This exercise can decrease scrap substantially. Moreover, the government must encourage people to establish green industries to curtail emissions.

The rising number of city dwellers is a pressing issue at various forums internationally and domestically. Therefore, individuals must work tirelessly in association with governments to deal with it timely and effectively.

268 Words

Vocab for Task – 43

1. reeling – winding / revolving
2. amenities – facilities
3. primarily - initially
4. contraceptives – preventives
5. depletion – exhaustion
6. hearing - enquiry
7. outrageous - shameful
8. commuters - travellers
9. deteriorating - worsening
10. snarl - growl
11. scattered – spread out
12. provinces - reign
13. holistic - complete
14. endeavour - attempt
15. sorting - categorisation
16. substantially - significantly
17. Adhering – listening carefully
18. Establish – set up
19. Curtail - limit
20. Emissions – give out
21. Dwellers - houses
22. Pressing – persistent
23. Tirelessly - untiringly

TASK 44

Some people believe that the government should take care of old people and provide financial support after they retire. Others say individuals should save during their working years to fund their own retirement. What is your opinion? Give reasons for your answer and include examples from your own experience.

Across the globe, administrations of numerous countries budget astronomical amounts to deliver medical and monetary assistance to retirees as a token of respect for their contribution to building the nation. However, some individuals believe that one must not exert a financial burden on the state exchequer by gathering resources during their productive years to save for retirement.

Since people have given their lives towards building the economic wealth of a nation, it is the turn of the state to provide for people on their retirement. It furthers the objective of being a utilitarian country by distributing resources equally among its population. These schemes furnish social security to the inhabitants, resulting in increased productivity of the young working residents. During advanced age, the chances of employment are reduced significantly. Thus, the administrations must ensure through welfare policies to provide sufficient means of support to elders for a dignified life as they have been paying taxes throughout their working years.

Contrastingly, we cannot disregard the significance of accumulating money to meet future needs. The savings provides freedom of spending money at retirement at the will of the person as one does not wait for the government funds. Besides, retirees will have sense of pride for not seeking benefits from the government at retirement.

I resonate with the fact that the established government is under a moral obligation to support its citizens after retirement. Government must provide financial support as it positively impacts mental health as people feel secure and independent in their post-work lives.

Personal circumstance of individuals may not allow them to save money to secure future. Therefore, it should be the duty of the elected government to safeguard its most vulnerable class of people by enacting laws that ensure their financial well-being.

292 Words

Vocab for Task -44

1. administration - management
2. retirees – senior citizen
3. monetary - financial
4. exchequer – treasury / government funds
5. furnish - supply
6. utilitarian - useful
7. inhabitants - citizens
8. ensure – to make sure
9. dignified - reputed
10. disregard - ignore
11. accumulating - gather
12. resonate - copy
13. enacting - acting
14. safeguard - protect
15. vulnerable - helpless
16. moral - ethical
17. obligation - compulsion

TASK 45

Some people assert that history has little value in the contemporary world. But some believe that history is needed today to learn from the past. Discuss both viewpoints and give your opinion. Give reasons for your answer and include any relevant examples from your own knowledge or experience.

Some individuals believe that history is insignificant in our modern world. Others consider that even though innovations are causing rapid changes to our present world, historical events significantly influence our current lives.

Across the globe, history is a dedicated subject in school curriculums. History offers insights to youngsters into the principles on which our community flourished in yesteryears. We must endeavour to protect historical places so that our coming ages can learn from the sufferings and achievements of our forefathers. Monuments depicting the aftermath of wars act as a deterrent for people in the present not to initiate arm conflicts, and sites portraying prosperity render motivation to achieve higher goals. Moreover, to appreciate the usages of customs and traditions, one must have full knowledge of our ancient backgrounds and scriptures. Medical know-how recorded in prehistoric books has paved the way for modern medicine and other technological fields.

On the contrary, many people believe that studying events in the past is an unworthy exercise as the knowledge of issues existing in the present world is more practical. They fiercely argue that the modern-day world has many complex difficulties for which our past actions cannot readily provide solutions. Besides, humans commit similar mistakes without learning a lesson, which negates the primary objective of history.

I reckon gaining knowledge of former times is indispensable as the decisions taken in the past by our ancestors become references for our contemporary and futuristic problems.

People interested in learning about the present working of society must comprehend its history. Accordingly, learning history has enormous significance in our current world, and everyone must strive to study it.

271 Words

Vocab for Task -45

1. assert - declare
2. contemporary - modern
3. insignificant – not important
4. dedicated - devoted
5. flourished - grow
6. insights – understandings / awareness
7. yesteryears – in past
8. endeavour - attempt
9. forefathers - ancestors
10. depicting - showing
11. aftermath - result
12. deterrent - restrain
13. initiate - start
14. portraying - representing
15. prosperity - wealth
16. render – cause to be
17. scriptures- holy bible
18. prehistoric - ancient
19. unworthy – not fit for
20. fiercely - violently
21. negate – contradict / undo
22. former - previous
23. indispensable - necessary
24. ancestors – predecessor in family
25. contemporary - modern
26. futuristic – ahead of its time
27. strive – attempt / struggle
28. enormous - huge
29. comprehend - understand

TASK 46

Many species of animals all around the world are on the verge of extinction. Some say that countries and individuals should protect these animals from dying out, while others say that we should concentrate more on the problems of human beings. Discuss both viewpoints and give your opinion. Give reasons for your answer and include any relevant examples from your own knowledge or experience.

Due to commercial reasons, various wildlife creatures are on the edge of extinction, which has gathered broad support for wildlife protection from several quarters. Contrarily, some individuals argue to concentrate more on problems faced by humans before committing resources for conserving animals.

The foremost importance of wildlife is that it is one of the essentials for the survival of human beings. Animals perform significant functions to facilitate agriculture by providing manure and helping in pollination. Numerous animals hold cultural and religious significance in many communities. I spent my childhood in Thailand, where elephants are considered deities. Ancient Thai texts describe Elephants to be the creature sent by God to help humans in war and peace. Therefore, the Thai public and government have taken large-scale measures to protect elephants from hunting and exploitation, which were on the brink of extinction at one point.

On the contrary, humanity is under extraordinary circumstances created by the depletion of non-renewable resources and global warming. We must preserve human life as homo sapiens are the most intelligent being in the food chain and have the power to resolve world problems with their intelligence. Many individuals in association with administrations are providing free food, shelter, and health services to conserve precious human lives. Besides, resolving problems faced by the human population will assist in creating sustainable environments for the coexistence of humans and wildlife.

Humans are transgressing over forests in the prospects of resources and habitation. Countless animal species have become extinct due to human greed. We depend on various animals for our essentials, such as food, clothing, and transportation. I reckon we must maintain an ecological balance by preserving our animal kingdom before focusing on other human problems.

Without animals, the civilisation of humans cannot survive and saving animals without resolving human problems will be unfruitful for humanity. Hence, we must strive to focus on both hardships, but we must first preserve our fauna as they are in existential crisis.

325 Words

Vocab for Task – 46

1. verge - edge
2. extinction - loss
3. contrarily – in counter
4. committing – carry out
5. pollination - fertilization
6. facilitate – enable / make possible
7. manure - dung
8. deities – worshipped being
9. brink - edge
10. exploitation - misuse
11. extraordinary - unusual
12. depletion - reduction
13. homo sapiens - humans
14. conserve - save
15. precious - valuable
16. coexistence – being at same time or place
17. transgress - misbehave
18. unfruitful - unproductive
19. fauna – animal kingdom
20. strive - attempt
21. existential – factual / pertaining to existence

TASK 47

Some people believe that schools should reward those students who show excellent academic performance while some believe that only the ones who show significant improvement in the grades should be rewarded. Discuss both the views and give your opinion. Give reasons for your answer and include any relevant examples from your own knowledge or experience.

Across the globe, students finishing at the top in academics are recognised. Since it is a more comfortable system, most institutions follow this traditional method. However, students making noteworthy improvements in academics are awarded rarely by institutions.

The foremost reason for acknowledging kids showing exponential growth is that even a small encouragement to them will have numerous positive effects on their psychological and academic results. This group will work with slight pressure and will be able to enjoy the learning experience. Appreciating students who show improvement will help them improve their social image among peers, thereby boosting their confidence. This reward system aspires other under-performing students to work hard to show significant improvement and earn recognition. This scheme not only shows appreciation for the students endeavouring to show improvement but is approval of the teacher's efforts.

On the contrary, we must not leave children excelling in examinations out of the rewarding system. We must ensure that extraordinary minds are recognised and appreciated for their hard work. The rewards for the struggle to accomplish academic excellence is necessary to keep students performing consistently on their tests. Furthermore, rewarding high scorers will create an extremely competitive studying environment at school and will result in higher overall grades.

I consider students with substantial improvements must receive accolades before top performers since their efforts are generally overlooked by our system.

The reward must not be discriminatory. Therefore, we must adopt a system which helps the goal of holistic academic development of every kind of student by rewarding them suitably.

255 Words

Vocab for Task -47

1. noteworthy - notable
2. exponential – at a rapid rate
3. slight - minor
4. aspire – seek / aim
5. appreciation - approval
6. endeavouring - aiming
7. excelling - outshining
8. consistently – time after time
9. accolade - honour
10. overlooked - ignored
11. discriminatory - biased
12. holistic - complete
13. suitably - well

TASK 48

In certain countries, the number of people who use bicycles as the main means of transport is decreasing even though it is beneficial both physically and environmentally. What can be the reasons for this change in preference? How can people be encouraged to use bicycles? Give reasons for your answer and include any relevant examples from your own knowledge or experience.

Across the globe, modes of transportation have improved exceptionally by innovations made by automobile technology. Despite having numerous advantages, the usage of bicycles as the primary method of conveyance is becoming obsolete with each passing day since it is one of the slowest means of mobility.

Since the introduction of mass transportation systems has lessened travel time significantly, people have stopped using bikes to save their precious time. The limited capacity of cycles to ferry passengers and cover long distances has caused a decline in their routine use. The auto industry has successfully manufactured fuel-efficient and low-polluting vehicles, which is one of the leading causes of diminution in the number of people using cycles.

With the high volume of small vehicles cumulating on roads, there is less space for bicycles resulting in fatal accidents. Mounting temperatures and global warming across major cities additionally make cycling unviable.

Governments should ensure radical steps to inspire people to encourage the use of cycles in their daily commute. A higher rate of taxes must be applied on motor cars to discourage buyer's from purchasing a new vehicle. Through awareness campaigns, the administration can spread information about the positive impacts of cycling on the environment and health. The creation of dedicated cycle tracks on the roads can provide safety to bicycle riders while on roads.

The use of bicycles must be promoted throughout the world, being the greenest transport since it assists in checking emission levels. Furthermore, it has the power to boost the overall health of people as it involves physical efforts.

258 Words

Vocab for task -48

1. exceptionally - extremely
2. conveyance - transportation
3. obsolete – out of date
4. mobility – ability to move
5. lessened - depleted
6. precious - valuable
7. ferry - ride
8. causes - justifications
9. diminution – decrease / reduction
10. cumulating - collecting
11. fatal - deadly
12. mounting - rising
13. radical – fundamental / essential
14. campaign - movement
15. dedicated - devoted
16. assist - help
17. checking - examine
18. boost - improve

TASK 49

Throughout history, people have dreamed of living in a perfect society, but they have not agreed on what an ideal society would be like. What do you think is the most important element of a perfect society in the modern world? How can people work towards achieving an ideal society?

Over the years, numerous philosophers have endeavoured to outline an idea of a model society. However, if we read history, none of the social scientists has been able to deliver a concept that could get acceptance by the masses.

Since every person has dissimilar aspirations and worldviews, none in the past has reached a consensus regarding what an ideal community should be. In the long history of humans, ambitions and lifestyles are continuously changing, which keeps the concept of a perfect world dynamic.

Contemporarily, the societies scoring higher on the index of living standards due to well-established human rights for their citizens is a model community to my beliefs. Residents must have equal opportunities and infrastructure without discrimination to live a dignified life through education, medical, and sanitation. The ecosystem of the civilisation must give prospects for equal work and wages for the realisation of aims and the self-esteem of all genders.

Therefore, the administration must strive to accomplish social justice by eliminating inequalities among the population based on sex, creed, and race. An idealistic civilisation should not confine itself to boundaries by restricting people from becoming its part and must follow a liberal policy on immigration, which will ensure diversity and socialising of distinct cultures. We should work to accomplish harmony with other nations by sharing our excess resources. It can be a significant footstep towards realising world peace and a favourable environment for creating perfect communities.

Humans may never reach a consensus regarding an ideal society. Nevertheless, we must channel our energies to impart knowledge to the young generation through schools and parents to respect diversity and strive for equality and social justice as a step toward an ideal society.

282 Words

Vocab for Task- 49

1. acceptance - recognition
2. dissimilar - different
3. aspiration - aim
4. consensus - agreement
5. ambition - goals
6. dynamic - lively
7. contemporarily - modern
8. discrimination - difference
9. dignified - noble
10. sanitation - hygiene
11. ecosystem - environment
12. civilisation - society
13. realisation - understanding
14. strive - attempt
15. eliminating - remove
16. inequalities - bias
17. consensus – general agreement
18. impart – pass on
19. strive - attempt

TASK 50

Some people think that the best way to improve road transport safety is to let the driver test each year. To what extent do you agree or disagree?

The number of fatalities entangled in vehicular accidents has soared, which has ignited the argument for reinventing road safety measures. Various individuals propose the best practice to ensure higher road safety is to put every driver on a refresher course each year to judge their capacity to drive and knowledge of traffic rules. However, my views are contrasting.

The proposal to test all drivers annually is not feasible since it may put financial and administrative burdens on the government. The monetary and human resource costs may not be fruitful as driving in the real world is entirely distinct from simulation and may not be able to judge the actual driving skills of the test taker. The test takers might be reluctant to test annually and might consider it a massive inconvenience in their time. Nevertheless, the best way to inculcate respect for road safety in citizens is by making them aware of traffic rules and regulations.

Authorities must display significant road safety signs, speed limits and any other rules alongside roads to assist commuters. Inclusion of the subject of transport safety in the school's academic curriculum will inculcate the culture of adhering to the norms of driving etiquette in our younger generation. Campaigns and distribution of material and knowledge through mass media on operating standards will make people aware of the significance of following road safety standards. Besides, officials must strictly implement the rules and regulations by imposing hefty fines on erring drivers. It will ensure the observance of road security protocols by citizens.

I reckon the safety of individuals needs more than just putting each driver to the test. Therefore, pragmatic steps to disseminate traffic laws can ensure the safety of citizens.

283 Words

Vocab for Task-50

1. fatalities – losses / deaths
2. entangled - complex
3. ignited - burning
4. argument - dispute
5. reinventing - recreate
6. feasible - possible
7. monetary - financial
8. entirely - completely
9. simulation - imitation
10. reluctant - unwilling
11. inconvenience - problem
12. inculcate - infuse
13. adhering - adhesive
14. norms - standard
15. etiquette - manners
16. implement - apply
17. imposing - commanding
18. hefty – heavy
19. erring - mistaken
20. observance - performance
21. pragmatic - realistic
22. disseminate – spread

Manufactured by Amazon.ca
Acheson, AB